girls!

Also by William Beausay

Boys!

girls!

Helping Your Little Girl
Become an Extraordinary Woman

Kathryn Beausay
& William Beausay

© 1996 by William Beausay and Kathryn Beausay

Published by Fleming H. Revell
a division of Baker Book House Company
P.O. Box 6287, Grand Rapids, MI 49516-6287

Spire edition published 2001

Fourth printing, April 2003

Printed in the United States of America

ISBN 0-8007-8683-1

Scripture is taken from the HOLY BIBLE, NEW INTERNATIONAL VERSION®. NIV®. Copyright © 1973, 1978, 1984 by International Bible Society. Used by permission of Zondervan Publishing House. All rights reserved.

TimeFraming, used on pages 209–12, is a registered trademark.

"The Window" on pages 116–18 is from *The Window and Other Essays* by G. W. Target. Copyright Pacific Press, Boise, Idaho. Used by permission.

For current information about all releases from Baker Book House, visit our web site:

http://www.bakerbooks.com

Contents

Preface

God made the world with its towering trees,
majestic mountains and restless seas, then paused
   and said,
"It needs one more thing—someone to laugh and dance
   and sing,
to walk in the woods and gather flowers,
to commune with nature in the quiet hours."
So God made little girls with laughing eyes and
   bouncing curls,
with joyful hearts and infectious smiles,
enchanting ways and feminine wiles,
and when he'd completed the task he'd begun
he was pleased and proud of the work he'd done.
For the world, when seen through little girls' eyes,
greatly resembles paradise.

Why God Made Little Girls
Author unknown

The topic of girls is so delightfully explosive, and we're so thankful to be lighting the wick! We've waited a long time to write this new, fresh map for developing excellent girls. It's been a journey for us but one that's led back to a practical and sensible style of childrearing. Simplicity always is best.

Have you ever met a young woman and been so impressed that you've said to yourself, *I've got to meet this girl's mother!* We have! In our experience as both professionals and parents, we've met many women who've demonstrated personal excellence through the firstfruits of their labors: their daughters.

We've taken an unusual step. We've asked several of those mothers to help us write this book! In the following pages you will find the heart and soul of these twenty-five women. They're just like the rest of us, representing a range of divergent economic, educational, ethnic, political, and religious persuasions. But one thread unites them: Each raised a girl that any of us would call a winner. These women are the *Girls!* Team, and you'll be hearing a lot from them. They've spawned and refined all of the pages you are about to read. They've guaranteed that this book would be smart, effective, and workable.

We are hardly ever going to mention boys in this book. You will, however, find yourself naturally comparing boys and girls many times. Your thoughts will run something like, *Well, I know boys who do the same things*, or *My son is just like that, too.* Girls and boys share all traits; however, some traits are more pronounced in girls than in boys. We would like to encourage you to think about girls on their own terms while reading this book. Many of the ideas we discuss could be applied to boys, but there's already a great book out on that topic! Girls are unique, and you would be wise to focus on those singular qualities defining them.

We have made this book practical. If you're expecting an extensive bibliographic analysis, doctoral level cunning, or various styles of intellectual swordplay, you're on the wrong bus! We have only one objective: to make our understanding of girls accessible to anyone wishing to help a girl seize her greatest potential. Parents who are devoted, capable, and inspired can do that.

For the purposes of this book, girls will be defined as those females who are aged four through the onset of puberty. Prior to that age they are babies, and after that time they are young women. Besides, this swath of life is large enough and easily complex enough to keep our tongues wagging and keyboards clattering for a long time.

We are delighted that you're joining us on this journey. We firmly believe that some things in life should simply be enjoyed. When it comes to simple enjoyment, raising girls is in a class by itself. Nothing in the world is more precious than the fountain of love and warmth bubbling from these lovely little creatures. Today brims with priceless moments we must stop and savor. This is your chance to make your little girl thankful she has you for a parent!

Acknowledgments

Creating a book like this requires the efforts and input of some key players. We've been blessed with not one but several of these folks who've acted not only as sounding boards but magnifiers as well. These friends have broadened and enriched our understanding by fearlessly sharpening our ideas and helping press out the wrinkles. We owe them each a sincere thanks.

Several stand out. First, thanks to Bill Petersen and his fine staff at Baker Book House. They've encouraged us along this entire trail and have been expert in helping capture our vision and love. Thanks as well to Steve and Marcia Milanowski, Frank and Carla Redmond, Elaine Heisman, and Karen and Matt Godsil. Your faithful friendship and encouragement over the years have blessed us. You've stimulated us to grow and think in new ways.

I (Kathi) am grateful to my parents, Jim and Dorothy Boulton, for providing me with a girlhood full of fun, love, and family times. Your continual love and encouragement has seen me through life's joys and struggles. Thanks for believing in me.

These acknowledgments wouldn't be complete without mentioning our real source of passion: Jake, Jessie, and Zac. Our love for you is beyond words. You all make us swell with pride, cry with concern, laugh with pleasure, and beam with

11

enjoyment. Whether you will ever change the world we don't know. All we know is that you've changed ours. Thank-you.

We'd like to offer a special thanks to all the women serving on the *Girls!* Team who contributed to this book. Through the eyes of you few we were able to see through the eyes of millions. You made plain to us what has been for a long time hidden, and we deeply appreciate your help. You will find your stories and yourselves here.

Members of the *Girls!* Team:

Dee Ann Scheider
Deborah Warner
Karen Godsil
Mary Rumschlag
Dorothy Boulton
Milane Beausay
Alice Rogers
Carol Derkin
Lorrie Fox
Leslie Boudouris
Dian Kwiatkowski
Linda Toepfer
Elaine Heisman
Lois Whitmer
Mary Kate Hafemann

Parental Discretion Advised

Girls! Girls! Girls!

There they were, perched like three chirpy little chickadees on our couch. They were colorful, bright, bubbly, and totally alive—my (Bill's) first little band of examinees ready to share with me the magic and mystery of girlhood! Oh sure, they were only seven years old and more adorable than cooperative, but so what? Inside these little women was the answer to a puzzling question I longed to answer: *What's it like to be a girl?* I just needed the right key to unlock the right vaults.

They initiated the talk. "If you want to know about girls, well, we love to laugh and fight," said the most excitable of the three. Being the fathead that I am, I scrambled to take notes on every word instead of interpreting the clear message that this would be a tough interview.

I replied very seriously, "I need you to tell me what it's like being a girl."

"You'll have to guess what, chicken butt!!" *Hee hee hee, hoo hoo, hee hee.*

I put my pen down. "Ahem. Let's try this again. . . . What do you most like about girlhood?"

"Nice try, chicken thigh!!" *Haaaa! haaaa! Hee hee hee, hoo hoo hoo, hee hoo haa.*

Strike two. This interview was beginning to feel like a car careening sideways on ice. But, hey, I'm a hip father of the '90s; I can go with the flow! *Let's just be cool and try this one more time,* I thought. *Maybe it's the timing of the questions.*

"So, what kinds of things do girls like to do?" I carefully plied.

"We do flips, chicken lips!!" *Ba, haaaaaaaaaaaaa!! Hee hee hoooo ha ha ha.*

Oh, man! My little darlings were reduced to a howling bevy of hyenas, rolling around on the couch in teary-eyed, gut-busting laughter, poking, slapping, and screeching—all at my expense. My understanding, my research, my knowledge all at stake. I was beat. Oh well, if you can't beat 'em, join 'em! *Yabba dabba doo! Hoo hoo!*

In the Beginning Was Dr. Spock

Dr. Benjamin Spock jumpstarted this whole childrearing business with an innocuous little book called *The Commonsense Book of Baby and Child Care* published in 1946. He successfully challenged parents from the perspective of a pediatrician genuinely concerned about how kids were being raised. As he first blazed the cliff-side trail on which we now creep, he inadvertently kicked the first stone in what's become a landslide of childrearing advice.

The avalanche has been crushing. Not to be outdone by the advice of a medical doctor, countless psychologists chipped in, then the psychoanalysts offered their cold stones, followed by the humanists of the '60s, the feminists of the '70s, the conservatives of the '80s, an assortment from the '90s, and wouldn't you know it, Dr. Spock again! What's ahead? Well, there's bad news and there's good news.

You're Just an Old Bag

There's a saying, "You don't know what's in a teabag until you put it in hot water." We're all in this childrearing teacup together. Due to the combined influences of the media, living close together, and public education, to name a few, we've been quietly submerged in a hot broth of ideas impacting us beyond our perception. It's only by looking at the long-term effects on our children that we can judge what kind of tea we've been.

The bad news is that our kids are having some problems. Though your daughter may not be struggling herself, she is a member of a society of imperiled children. Never in the history of this country have so many children been given so many material things, yet they have failed to develop inner character. Our children are floundering because of problems related to family life, parental involvement, cultural values, and conflicting commitments.

Here's the good news: The problems facing kids today are fixable. At the time of this writing, we as a society are undergoing a new shift in adult attitudes toward families. Women are clearly experiencing an urge to be home. They've witnessed that what's been sacrificed by choosing the career track is irreplaceable. Fathers too are finding to their surprise that family life is quite agreeable and in fact desirable. These are wonderful trends for which we should be thankful.

The specific forces affecting mothers are different from those affecting fathers. The best way to address them is for us to have private chats with both Mom and Dad. Ladies first.

Mother . . . Please Relax and Listen

We see these five specific forces impacting mothers today:

1. A lack of confidence created by the unclear role of mothers
2. Being overly cautious in raising girls

3. The idea that, to succeed, girls must be better than boys
4. The belief that complex answers are better than common sense
5. An inability to be fresh and flexible

Today women are confused about their roles as women and mothers. The confusion arises from the myriad of conflicting options ranging from career opportunities to stay-at-home motherhood. In addition to conflicting options are conflicting expectations: being a wonderful mother, assertive career woman, Cindy Crawford look-alike, PTA president, and soccer coach. This "super-woman" expectation has eroded our natural confidence in being great mothers.

Whether you are a dedicated career woman or a stay-homie, your role is secondary to the attitudes you communicate about your role. Each generation of mothers has different role choices to make, and girls have always survived the shifts and changes. So will yours. Be confident and optimistic despite whatever hidden role-pressure you may feel.

Closely linked to an eroded confidence base is excessive caution in raising girls. We cannot possibly know all the walls our girl will smack into on her trip through life, and that terrorizes us. Here's an alternate and more realistic view: Girls were made for this rough-and-tumble world and outfitted for trouble. We must raise them with an expectation and a self-confidence that they will prevail. We must expose them to challenge and difficulty—and yes, even to fear.

Girls need life-threatening, fearful things in their lives for good mental health. *What*?! Such a proposal sounds ghastly by today's standards! Unfortunately, girls will never learn to handle the good and bad in life unless we let them touch it.

If there is one droning, redundant theme we constantly hear and read it is the notion that in order to be successful, girls need to be better than boys. Please expunge this idea from your head! Boys are a universe of their own and have nothing to do with raising girls and much less with being a standard of comparison. Girls are fabulous on their own terms, and we need to begin thinking about them in relation to themselves.

Our culture seems to believe complex answers are better or more correct than simple ones. Avoid this trap. The more complicated parenting solutions become, the more error-prone they are. Bloated, scientific-sounding schemes for raising kids are simply foolish. Let's keep our thinking simple.

We are bombarded with cultural influences telling us what to do and what to think. Nobody *needs* his or her own ideas. We've become intoxicated with predigested ideas and answers for everything. These ideas and answers are slowly poisoning our God-breathed ability to think and act for ourselves with originality and flexibility. Counteract these forces with the following ideas:

- Cultivate passionate wishes for your daughter
- Avoid the extremes
- Model inner beauty and grace
- Learn to be a gentle friend and compassionate listener
- Celebrate and participate in your daughter's girlhood

Passionate Wishes

Your daughter is a wonderful, beautiful, and talented expression of God's grace in your life. Be thankful for her daily and enjoy the natural pride swelling automatically within you! We have no doubt that she's brought you immense happiness and satisfaction way beyond our pitiful efforts to describe. We want you to bubble with excitement when you stop to ponder how blessed you are.

There is no shortage of books encouraging you to let your girl "find her own way" in life. But this seems so unnatural! We've never met a mother who simply lets her girl bop along. No! We all want our girls to stand out, to establish themselves in some extra-special way, as extra-special as we feel they are. We pray and wish for them to be confident, strong, full of self-respect and conviction. And we're willing to do anything necessary to get them there.

Don't surrender your deepest wishes for your girl, no matter who suggests otherwise. Having challenging aspirations for our daughters is fantastic! Believing in extraordinary girls is something we wish to encourage.

Every girl needs at least one crazy person in her life who believes that her wishes can come true, no matter how insane those wishes might seem. Be the nutty person who tells her she can do anything. Shout it loudly and often. Say it proudly! Don't get economical on your enthusiasm.

Think about this story. We met a girl at a traveling fair passing through our town. She was eight years old, and we found her playing with a diesel engine that ran a clattering little merry-go-round operated by her parents. She was pathetic. The contrast between her and the girls in our group was stark—they were bright and cheery and she, gray and vacant . . . and gulping diesel fumes by the cubic yard.

What struck us was how easy she was to ignore. It was as if her lack of personality made her somehow invisible. Had she not been sitting next to an exhaust pipe, we might not have even noticed her. We quickly became preoccupied with saving her life! We hailed her over and stumbled through a difficult conversation, gathering some sad details. She was an only child, lived in a panel truck, was home schooled, and was clearly uncomfortable with speaking to us.

As we talked to the girl, it began to rain. We suggested she run for cover, but her mother (she was a worst-case-scenario mother—words fail to capture her) yelled from behind us, "Aww, she's just a filthy little weed! She needs a little waterin'!" Then, glaring at her girl, she spit, "Get back over there where you were at!"

It's sad to think that this lonely little traveler is going to assault life like all the rest of our daughters without even the vaguest hope of much achievement. We all share the tug of despair knowing that she will probably not achieve excellence. She is a deep well of possibility, fouled by her parents' lack of vision.

We all have our own feelings toward mothers like this, but are you really any different? Now don't gasp! Think it through. Is thinking big, crazy things for your girl an active, daily priority? Have you decided to act in continually positive ways toward your girl? Are you thoughtful and diligent? We must choose to think this way, and most of us haven't learned to consciously choose these thoughts.

Many of us come from backgrounds where life just "happened" to us. We're unfamiliar with making a decision, setting a goal, and going after it relentlessly. Any mother can decide to wish passionately for her girl, but so few do. You need to become part of a select group of mothers making daily decisions to help their daughters reach high.

Avoid the Extremes

Think about this: Seven of ten pregnancies are accidents. Two of ten children are conceived despite the use of contraception. One of ten are planned and wanted. You may have had good reasons for having your daughter, or (like the other seven of us) may have had no reason at all! Your reasons for having your daughter can determine your child-rearing attitudes.

There are two extremes here. One extreme is raising a daughter exclusively for our sake: Girls in this scenario are little more than helpers and assistants. The other extreme is raising a daughter exclusively for her sake, turning her into a full-blown prima donna. Nothing is required of this girl. Both extremes are precarious in their own way.

The *Girls!* Team has spoken. The best spot to raise winning girls is not on either extreme, but somewhere on the prima donna side of center. If you occupy one of the fringes, please consider the long-term results. "Your" girl is simply in your care here. Raise her for her own sake while giving her a balanced life.

Inner Beauty and Grace

Mothers spill into their daughters all their special feminine ways. Daughters soak it up with a natural absorbency, mimicking gestures, posture, voice, and mannerisms. As girls get older, they're aware of how mothers dress and do their hair. You've no doubt accidentally caught your girl in the midst of her own form of role-playing. She's probably wanted to help you with your hair, let you know what she thinks you should wear, and she's ended up dressing a lot like you.

Daughters model inward beauty just as fastidiously. A girl mimics her mother's attitudes, contentedness with herself, optimism, strength, wisdom, patience, gentleness, and sense of humor. Developing these positive qualities is your role. Take a mental measurement of yourself. What you transmit affects what she sees in herself. Remember, a big pair of eyes is watching you.

You are her standard of beauty and grace. Do what you can to set a high mark. Tell her specifically what her endearing qualities are, what's especially important to you, and what you love and admire the most. Make a special effort to mention the physical qualities that make her unique.

A Gentle Friend and Compassionate Listener

You can easily be your daughter's most treasured and trusted confidante. One of our *Girls!* Team members remarked that she was most excited to have a girl because she needed a "partner in crime." By virtue of your position as Mom comes the natural opportunity to share your daughter's doubts, concerns, accomplishments, and ideas. You've traveled down her road before and you can best show your love by stopping, stooping, and listening. Let her open up and run on. Just follow where she goes. At the end of the listening trip sits a pot of gold—a treasure called closeness.

Celebrate Her Girlhood

George MacDonald said, "There are some things worth being a child to get ahold of again." This world of girls is such an inspiring, thrilling place! Join your daughter and live in her world. Don't sit off in the background like some plant; grab a Barbie and dive in! There's nothing like a little fun to liven up a dull adulthood!

Daddy, Are You Still with Us?

There's a big secret we men must concede: Our lives are spent in self-absorption. We invest most of our time thinking about ourselves and the job we're doing, how we compare to Jack the banana salesman next door, and what's in life for us.

Crashing this tightly guarded ego party come women— and daughters! And the game of life suddenly snaps to a different beat. This scene replays itself daily and constitutes for us guys one of life's great challenges: *Trying to understand girls!*

We're great at guessing about girls and proclaiming that we understand them. But let's face it, it's rare when we get more than a tiny pinch of understanding. But do you think we'd ever admit it? No way! We'll just continue privately praying for a miracle that girls might somehow make sense to us.

That reminds me (Bill) of a story. I was once counseling a rather dispirited man who was in the midst of a nasty divorce. He had two daughters (ages five and seven) living with his ex-wife, and he wasn't allowed visitation very often. He wanted to appear to his wife to know all about girls, so he read *Seventeen* and *Teen* magazines to find out what girls liked to do. After all this high-powered research, he just couldn't understand why his girls wanted to play dolls (he hadn't read about that in any of his sources) or why it upset his wife when he let his daughters listen to wild rock music and go makeup shopping at the local department stores. And the tattoos—whoa! They really set her off!

Most fathers, like him, have trouble understanding girls. But do we guys ever ask for directions? Do we ask for help? No! We're more defensive than the Dallas Cowboys and under no circumstances would we ask for guidance. This attitude leads to mistakes, misunderstandings, and meandering.

Understanding your wife and daughter is not as crucial as *wanting* and *trying* to understand them. That's all you need, especially with your daughter. Begin that process by reviewing this list of status quo thoughts of the fathers of the '90s:

- Just buck up, baby
- Passion has no place in parenting
- I needn't act in any special way; girls are no big deal
- Just set high standards and make her work to reach them
- You raise the girls; I'll raise the boys

Just Buck Up, Baby

Many fathers have a "buck-up" approach to raising kids. Their perspective goes something like this: "I was given a kick in the teeth when I was young, and if I came out all right, so will they! So no more goofball parenting ideas!"

This is a double-edged philosophy. On the good edge, we must ignore kooky parenting ideas. Any man with a wife who reads too many parenting books knows what we mean! On the bad edge, too many dads are excusing themselves from raising their girls. Be honest with yourself. Be sure you're not wounding your daughter because you're too lazy to read and learn!

Passionate Parenting

Most girls don't know any "live" men. The men they know are pressured and preoccupied, with no time for real living, no time for real zeal for life, let alone time for them. Just well dressed, manicured, and cologned corpses, as far as they can tell. Don't let passionate fatherhood escape you. Act quickly while you can.

Get fired up! The next few chapters might inspire some adventures you can have with your girl. You only have one go-around in girlhood, so make it count! The time is now.

No Big Deal

Many fathers believe they needn't do anything really special to raise a great girl. We maintain that if you want average girls, do average things. If you want exceptional girls, do exceptional things. What those exceptional things are will unfold in the pages of this book. Make your choice.

High Standards

There is everything good about setting high standards for your girl to live up to. What's wrong is thinking that all you must do is set high standards, then step away. That approach has a 1 percent success rate. Fathers must coach their daughters and show them how to climb. Pointing and saying in effect, "Go fetch" doesn't cut it—not if you want your girl to succeed. You are her guide. You can richly enhance her chances of success.

Dad's Role

Does the "You raise the girls, I'll raise the boys" proposal sound familiar? Your role in your daughter's life is enormous, and largely unseen. The *Girls!* Team members are unanimous in believing that fathers can teach daughters such things as the work ethic, self-confidence, and assertiveness. You provide a model of how men should relate to women. Your modeling becomes her guide for male relationships.

Interestingly, the *Girls!* Team also told us that as little girls they all wanted to spend more time with their dads. There was near unanimous agreement that most of the special memories of girlhood revolved around things done with Dad. You are vital to your daughter now and you will break her heart if you don't make her a priority in your life.

Here are some suggestions for building a foundation on which you and your daughter can grow and blossom together.

Learn how girls experience the world. If this book has one stated objective it is to somehow, someway allow you to experience first-hand what it must be like to be a girl. Knowing what that's like will permit you to feed your daughter's needs in new ways. By permitting yourself some creative latitude, you'll learn more than you ever thought you could know about being a girl.

Measure time in length, not weight. We want to make your girl so irresistible that you want to spend time with her—not just the vaunted *quality time*, but special, magical moments. Logging time with your daughter proves her value to you and sets her standards for future relationships with men. We've also seen that the closer a girl is to her dad, the better will be her chances of success as a woman.

Think about her when you're not with her. This is a simple act communicating an intense message. Make reminders to yourself to think about her, pray for her, write notes to her. Tell her you've done so. A special feeling grows in the heart of a little girl who knows that the man in her life was thinking of her. It's called "love."

New habits will be second nature when you've finished this book. You'll learn the overwhelming power of notes, secrets, private languages, special dates, and public demonstrations of affection and fondness, and will find many opportunities to practice them. Start now and get a jump on the fun!

Recognize her beauty. Little girls love to be noticed, especially by their mothers and fathers. But there's magic when it's Dad. It intensifies her belief in herself to have her beauty noticed. You need to learn how to jump through that fleeting window of opportunity.

Be the source of her stability. Resolve in your mind to remain the symbol of stability. Remember that your girl is sensitive to the problems and difficulties you face, whether or not she lets you know she's watching. She needs assurances that everything will be all right; i.e., you are not going to fall apart and leave her. She'll look for that type of stability in you, and it works out best all around if you can provide it.

If you've already fumbled this duty, don't despair. Just pick up the pieces now and commit to doing the best you can. Get your personal house in order—your marriage, your finances, and your emotions. It's never too late, especially for the man committed to being his very best. Forget your past and move now!

Be one of her true believers. Be the person in your girl's life who is wildly optimistic about her chances for success. Concentrate on all her good qualities. Be sickeningly optimistic and energized, carbonated beyond recognition! Blast her with hope! Suggest she tear apart and rebuild lawnmower engines, paint a portrait, build a birdhouse, do chemistry experiments! Do wild things to prove your utter blind faith in her, and make believing in the impossible the most fun a father and daughter can have.

Part 1

What Are Normal Girls and What Do They Do?

Created to Win

The Story of My Cool Pen

I (Bill) used to have this gorgeous Mont Blanc pen, one of those really expensive ball-point jobbies. All the cool authors used them, and I was so proud of it. It made me feel like Mr. Pulitzer. I had an interesting experience with that pen before I lost it.

We did many great things together. I signed my greatest checks with it. I scribbled timeless shopping lists with it. I underlined my Bible with it! It knew me and was so smart it could almost take dictation. Nobody could do with my pen the things I could do!

Till one day my artist brother-in-law Matt asked to borrow it. I discovered my pen had a side I never knew about. The pictures it created were beyond anything I ever imagined it capable of doing. If what I did made it write, what Matt did made it *live!* It was always capable of those things, I guess, but it took the hand of an artist to reveal its best nature. I felt ashamed and stupid, and later apologized to my pen for being such a generic slob. It escaped from me one day, disappearing at a busy convention, probably trying to get back to Matt's house!

Her Gifts

Your girl's a winner! We're often asked, What do you mean by "winner"? Your daughter was born with all the qualities of a true champion. Consider this sample list:

> Willingness to help others
> Willingness to serve
> Physical toughness
> Laughter
> Intellectual curiosity
> Intelligence
> Gifts in sports, music, artistry, interpersonal skills
> An ability to listen and follow advice
> Internal guidance/moral reliance
> Ambition (a desire to get better) and a means to achieve

This is the factory direct, base model girl. Varying amounts of each quality make the difference between girls. We consider these inborn features to be the attributes of winners. But as with my pen, what happens to these qualities rests heavily on the one who possesses them.

Her Greatest Gift

There are some aspects of your daughter you can't change. But you should ask, "If I can't change everything, what can I change?" The answer to this question is *you*.

For whatever reason, you are the one who's been given the opportunity to play a focal role in the development of a young, independent life. You are the most crucial gift this girl has, and we must spend a small amount of time developing you for this once-in-a-lifetime opportunity.

What's a Winning Parent?

We were once in a mall, and I (Bill) was very tired of walking, so I sat down to peoplewatch. I saw the usual tall ones, short ones, round ones. Along came a sloppily dressed fella, limping slightly, with his small daughter in tow. They took a seat next to me, and we all said hello to each other. He was kind of an amazing guy, and the way he interacted with his daughter was heartwarming.

He appeared mentally slow and, frankly, was difficult to understand. He chattered with his little girl, complimented her on her curls, straightened her dress, and sang her some songs. He was charming to watch. He was setting a new standard for me.

Ever researching, I was dying to ask this guy some questions. When it seemed proper, I opened with, "She sure is the apple of your eye!" He leaned over toward me and with a gleam I shall never forget said, "She's my angel."

"I don't get to see many fathers that pay such attention to their girls," I plied.

"You don't? . . . Maybe you should hang around me more!" he shot back. I chuckled and said, "What's the secret to raising happy girls?"

He got serious, looked down at his twisted feet, then looked back at me squarely. He said simply, "You only get one shot, buddy. Just do your best every single minute."

I think that maybe for a moment on that summer afternoon in the mall, I got to talk to one of God's real men.

Girls are born with a blend of qualities necessitating great care in development. It's not difficult to identify each of these qualities, but harmonizing them takes some craft. Conducting such a development requires parents with knowledge and skills, proper attitudes, and determination. This combination isn't an accident. Skilled parents are the product of actual experience. Unfortunately, as we all know, when we have enough experience to be good parents, we're grandparents!

We need a way to have the seasoned experience and knowledge of a veteran mom and dad when we are young enough to influence our children's lives. The best place to begin is by comparing what parents say they want for their girls with what parents actually need for their girls.

What Do Parents Want?

Parents generally *want* their little girl to be protected and safe, be happy and fulfilled, develop close friendships, do well in school, have cool birthday parties, and smell nice.

Chances are that what you *need* in order to get your daughter these things is not clear in your mind. You're not alone; being unaware of the specific steps is normal. Raising girls is often like a puzzle without all the pieces, a treasure map with no lines, a mystery with too few clues. Let's examine the specific wants to see if we can discover what we're going to need.

Our research yielded some specific wants of parents of girls. Perhaps our most profound discovery is that *we all want the same things for our girls:*

> Physical safety
> The ability to communicate openly
> Self-confidence, good self-image, and self-esteem
> Happiness
> A positive outlook
> Self-discipline
> A unique and well-defined personality
> To be socially well-adjusted
> Resourcefulness
> To be industrious and capable of supporting themselves
> Cleverness and creativity
> Intelligence
> The ability to relate well with boys and adults
> The ability to express their talents and gifts
> Logical, clear thinking

Good decision-making skills
Good sense and wisdom
The ability to decide a moral direction and live it
The ability to laugh—hard
Solid friendships
Contentment
Attractiveness
Good health
Noble aspirations
A substantive relationship with God
To be well-rounded
Joy
To have a love for life
Intuition
To be poised
The ability to ask for what they want
The ability to recognize their own uniqueness
A good education
To be energetic
To be risk-takers

Wanting these things for our daughters and having the know-how needed to develop them are distinctly different. Developing the know-how is your responsibility.

How Do We Get What We Want for Our Girls?

I must tell you about one of the most interesting clients I ever worked with. I met him in an office that had a large chalkboard on the wall. Our session started with his going to the board and drawing two circles, a smaller one inside a much larger one, like this:

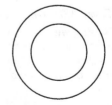

Apparently, he had it in his mind to lecture me, and I didn't stop him. *This should be interesting,* I cackled to myself.

He told me that the bigger circle represented everything in the world that we know right now: our names and personal history, facts and figures learned in school, experiences, opinions—everything. Inside this big circle was a smaller circle, representing all the stuff that we don't know but that we know we don't know. For instance, you might not know the calculations for Einstein's special theory of relativity, but you know you don't know it. Such information would be inside the little circle.

Then he stepped away from the chalkboard and drew large circles in the air between us and around us. "Do you know what's out here?" he asked in a reverent whisper.

"Uh, no. No, I don't," I quietly replied, trying to imitate his whisper and gag back the laughter.

He went back to the chalkboard and pointed to the area around the circle and said, "This is what we don't know we don't know!"

My sneering abruptly stopped. I sat there for a minute mesmerized by what he had said. It made terrific sense to me! I saw that there is a whole lot of information available to us that we don't know even exists. It's out there, but we aren't even aware of it!

Some of the best insight and wisdom in this book originate in the area of what you don't know you don't know. Expect it.

Seven Winning Attitudes

Raising winning girls starts by having winning attitudes. Developing these seven attitudes will hold you secure when the waves of life are pounding hard. They'll guide you when you're confused about what to do next.

1. Nothing works all the time, so relax.
2. Don't quit.

3. Create momentum.
4. Be an encourager.
5. Don't become weary of doing good.
6. Open yourself up to serendipity.
7. Love her enough to die for her.

1. Nothing works all the time. We pay lots of money for books and knowledge, so we naturally assume what we learn ought to work, right? Wrong. The lesson we've learned is that nothing works all the time. Nothing. Don't labor under the notion that scientifically validated parenting techniques and ideas always do anything. Real-life experience tells us that nothing is so consistent. Plan on being creative in the application of ideas and suggestions in the inevitable event that a cherished or promising technique flops.

2. Don't quit. I once heard some wonderful wisdom from an old-time football coach: "I have known many great people who have become mediocre by an inability to accept and abide by a defeat. If you should develop any success and develop superior qualities, chances are it will be because of the manner in which you meet the defeats that come to you, as they come to everyone." You will meet defeats on the road to raising your girl. If you're successful, chances are it will be because of your refusal to surrender to the complexity of it all. When the difficulties and problems arise, and they will, be more determined, read more, think more, ask more questions, and never give up!

3. Create momentum. We try to start each day with a short list of ideas orienting our daughter to the future, such as, "Something great's going to happen to you today!" or "You're going to learn something today that you will remember for thirty years!" or even "Play hard, honey. You can't make any mistakes we can't fix!" We want to get her life and thoughts moving in a good, positive direction.

4. Be an encourager. Be the Norman Vincent Peale of your daughter's existence! We make it a point to lift girls up no matter how goofy or corny we might sound. We try to be the most positive people our girl knows. We like it that way! We know that such an attitude accomplishes work deep in the hearts of little girls.

5. *Don't become weary of doing good.* Attitudes get tired. Carefully guard your good attitudes because you will be blitzed daily with reasons to surrender. If you don't surrender, you will find your good attitudes and good works reaping benefits.

6. *Open yourself up to serendipity.* Serendipity is finding the surprising, unexpected happenings in day-to-day life. Nike, the athletic footware manufacturer, spent millions of dollars developing its famous slogan about what to do. The magic of that phrase is that when you "just do it," anything might happen. Don't do it, and little or nothing is going to happen. Be ready for anything and you'll be amazed what serendipity happens for you and your daughter.

7. *Love her enough to die for her.* This is a pretty special kind of love not seen much these days—even in parents. We strongly urge you to think your daughter more important than yourself! Be willing, if necessary, to put her needs in front of any of yours. This won't make her selfish or self-centered. It will help her feel secure and confident. We recommend a completely selfless attitude born of a desire to make your daughter something very special. She is.

"Maybe" Isn't Good Enough

I (Kathi) leased a new car from a close friend once. I was the lukewarm buyer salespeople really hate. I couldn't decide what to do, so my friend the salesman agreed to let me think it over. Being the great salesman that he is, he left me with a powerful thought: "Kathi, I can take a yes and I can take a no, but a maybe will kill me." Being a practical person myself, I knew exactly what he meant. A yes means a sale, a no means forget it and move on to the next buyer, but a maybe means nothing. Limbo. Stuck. *Maybes* clog up the world.

You can get what you need to raise your daughter to excellence on one condition. You must say to yourself, *Yes, excellence is what she needs and I will do anything necessary to get it!* That's the kind of ironclad willpower that allows parents to give their children something of great quality.

Or you can say, *No, excellence is not what I need for my girl, and I will not try to get it.* At least this position shows some decisiveness and is a position that, though misguided, is clear.

Whatever you do, don't say, *Maybe. Maybes* handicap children. Don't be a fence sitter. Putting off the decision to do something about your girl's excellence is equivalent to a no.

Ruby Slippers

As you practice and learn, your girl-raising talent will slowly be fit with a new perspective, much like a pair of shoes. Time, effort, and patience intermingle to create a seasoned parent. But like Dorothy in *The Wizard of Oz*, you must act.

As you will recall, at the end of that story Dorothy learned that her ruby slippers could have flown her back to Kansas at any time. She wouldn't have listened even if she had been told, because she wasn't ready to go home! She needed to fight a green witch and little flying chimps to change her attitude. It worked. And when she was ready, she clicked her heels and got swooshed back without a hitch.

The greatest, most dazzling information in all the world is limp and lifeless without someone to apply it. But you can't be pushed, cajoled, or tricked into action. We know that. So, whenever *you're* ready, click on!

The Development Game

One of our *Girls!* Team members remarked, after having her fourth child, that though she isn't an expert on having newborns, she knows what she *can't* do. She can't make them sleep when she's tired, she can't make them stop barfing, she can't make them use fewer diapers, and she can't get her husband to wake up at night!

There's really only one good reason to do a chapter like this: *By understanding the sequence of development, you can more effectively determine what you can change and what you can do nothing about.* The facts of biological development are 99.9 percent nonsense-free because they've been observed to be reliable. The facts are predictable and almost totally invariable over many generations.

The details of child development are voluminous. What you need to know isn't. There are two levels of biological development, one that you can see physically and one that you see only in behavior. As a general rule, we tend to be less interested in physical development and more interested in behavioral changes. This tendency is probably related to the belief that we can't influence physical development much but can do something about behavior. It's important to briefly skim both areas and see how they interact with each other.

She's a Miracle

Let's quickly review the development scenario as seen from the perspective of a female embryo. She's created from a galactic number of potential genetic combinations. There is nobody else exactly like her. She is a miracle, and her conception begins a well-sequenced parade of developments.

Over the first nine months, this magnificent creature grows and develops at a rapid rate, growing two million percent from conception to the eighth week! At three weeks, the eyes form and the heart flutters for the first time. A rudimentary brain along with the five physical senses form by eight weeks, and preferences in light, sound, taste, and touch develop quickly thereafter. Differentiation of the most important organ and physiological systems (arms, legs, fingers, blood vessels, nerves, liver, gallbladder, and intestinal tract to name just a few) is completed during this time period, rendering her recognizable as a tiny, functioning human being.

And she has two inborn mysteries that science cannot capture nor common sense fathom: life and girlness. No matter how much we try, isolating the essence of life is impossible. Mankind has tried desperately to find it, only to fail repeatedly. Scientists can completely disassemble a frog down to its component parts and then reconstruct it. When finished, they'd have lying before them a complete and perfectly rebuilt frog. But one thing would be missing: life. Where did it go? What is it? Life, it seems, is a coy, fleeting thing sprinkled into us like pixie dust.

Like life, girlness hides her shiny face right in front of us! Perhaps we're being naive to even attempt defining her. Perhaps it's just wise to take a deep, reverent breath and sit quietly admiring in awe. Girlness is God-breathed.

A Predictable Sequence

All children pass through a predictable sequence of physical development that does not vary from the route, ever. The speed at which your daughter dashes through may be different, but the sequence of steps is the same for all girls. You can rest assured that whatever level of development your daughter is currently traversing will in time be concluded, leading lock-step to another.

Physical Changes You Can See

Normal baby girls are born pre-programmed to grow to reproductive maturity within ten to fourteen years. This development involves for the most part physical changes happening rapidly at first (birth to five years), slowing in the middle years, then accelerating as adolescence nears. Bone, muscle, immune system, and organ growth accelerate at birth.

Following closely behind is central nervous system development, which grows in a different way. A child is born with all the neurons (brain cells) she will ever have. Development of sensory and cognitive abilities is highlighted, not by the growth of new tissue, but by the elaborate interconnections created between the existing cells. These connections build rapidly at first, then slow into a more steady course of development, speeding again around age six, then settling back into a more even growth pattern.

Girls continue growing with no outside direction. A girl's body "knows" how to get exactly what it needs to proceed forward to completion.

How does it know? All babies are designed to survive by being comfort seekers. That trait never leaves them and in fact becomes more intense and specific over time. Baby girls are gifted with the ability to seek sustenance and protection, develop highly specific preferences, and make choices. These abilities are formed, mind you, prior to birth! These are the dominating impulses that later drive a baby's crying, moving, struggling, eating, and reflexes.

Changes You Can See in Behavior

Your daughter's growth and changes are a lot like those popular hologram pictures. Looking carefully you see only inconsequential nonsense! Then suddenly you see a stunning three-dimensional image.

Think of your daughter as one of these pictures. Look long and carefully. Three distinct and clear images coalesce as we view the splotchy outward image of her development. The merging images are those of brains, feelings, and friends (cognition, emotions, social development). Let's take a closer peek at each.

Bright, Bubbly Brains!

Girls move from birth (a period of complete sensory dependence with no ability to think logically) to maturity (fully logical and able to think abstractly) in four stages spanning twelve years, more or less. Stage one is that of being sensory bound, unable to effectively think but rather focused steadfastly on what can be experienced through sight, sound, touch, taste, and smell. Girls have only a slowly emerging sense of personal boundaries at this time, which means they start off not knowing where their skin stops and the rest of the world begins! They are also beginning to display a trait they carry with them through all life: a preoccupation with human faces. This sensory stage lasts until approximately twenty-four months of age.

Stage two runs approximately from ages two to six when girls figure out the world by playing with it. They test everything. Girls at this age are dominated by curiosity about things around them, and though learning to speak, spend most of their waking hours actively engaged in physical manipulation of toys and objects. Their low pain threshold makes them sensitive to touch and easily intimidated by sensory overload of all types, including yelling. Habits, *and the ability to create them,* begin here, and some of these can last a lifetime.

Stage three begins at about ages five to seven and goes to ages ten to twelve. At this stage girls are able to roughly assume the perspective of another person. They have developed intuition and a sophisticated ability to understand social rules and right and wrong. With this mental ability comes that of keeping—or hiding—information from you.

In stage four, beginning between the ages of 10 and 12, we see our girl's first real facility with cause and effect and logic. She also begins to grasp the meaning of abstract concepts like love, devotion, and hypocrisy. This is the start of complex reasoning and moral decision making at an adult level. This stage brings self-realization—a girl becomes aware that she has a body and actually exists in time and space apart from everyone else. Her use of language is also blossoming. She's able to express her thoughts and make her wishes known.

Whew! That was fast! Please appreciate that the ages here are approximations; there's a lot of variation in when these developments happen, but not in their order.

Emotions

Let's call the second 3-D image "emotional development." For those of you familiar with emotions, the idea that they develop in any rational way sounds oxymoronic. The creation of emotions makes sense to the extent that it fits into what the body is naturally trying to achieve: survival. Emotions are tools that help the body survive. Emotions are inborn motivators for seeking comfort, safety, and security.

Emotional development has a number of important features. First, emotions fluctuate wildly. Believe it or not, emotions are the most wild and unpredictable when a girl is very little. Little girls throw temper tantrums as easily as they smile and laugh. Emerging maturity, however, plays complex games with emotions. It's difficult to learn logic and abstract reasoning. Combine this with the dizzying chemical changes of this age, and emotions become difficult to predict.

Second, girls become increasingly able to perceive the emotions of others. They quickly read your vocal inflections and body and facial movements. This perception is probably related to a general drive in girls to seek connections with others. Healthy emotional development appears to be closely related to the quality of those connections.

Third, as girls mature, they have an increasing need to be recognized by others. They will go to whatever length necessary to matter to someone, using a variety of interpersonal skills. Don't bother asking your daughter about this behavior; she will not be able to explain it at all. But she needs to have mother, father, and special friends recognize her as a distinct, special human being. This is a natural drive for her, and something you should try to satisfy.

Now, Social Development

Nothing gives parents fits like the third hologram image. For that reason we'll spend the most time here. Social development is somewhat age dependent. Each year of age brings with it different challenges that will keep you scrambling.

Girls evolve their own culture. This culture has stunning detail and complex rules explaining many of what are otherwise confusing behaviors. The culture of girlhood is held together by three major elements. First, girls are constantly seeking sameness and a give-and-take balance (referred to as "symmetry") in their relationships with others; second, girls naturally want to give life to inanimate objects; and third, their growing sense of self-awareness determines the choices they make.

Intimacy through Symmetry

Symmetry is when something is alike on both sides. Faces have symmetry because either half is a reflection of the other. Symmetry describes what girls seek in their relationships with one another: They want to reflect each other's thoughts and feelings. Why? Because this creates intimacy. And girls will do almost anything for intimacy.

Deborah Tannen uses this concept brilliantly, and in her book *You Just Don't Understand* says women approach the world

> as an individual in a network of connections. In this world, conversations are negotiations for closeness in which people try to seek and give confirmation and support, and to reach consensus. They try to protect themselves from others' attempts to push them away. Life, then, is a community, a struggle to preserve intimacy and avoid isolation. Though there are hierarchies in this world . . . they are hierarchies more of friendship than of power and accomplishment.[1]

Women invoke a sophisticated set of language and other communication skills to achieve symmetrical relationships. These skills are mastered as little girls.

This development of relationships can be best illustrated with money. In our financial economy, we purchase things of value to us by trading money. Dollars are the power to make things happen. In a girl's social economy, the equivalent of dollars is talking and relating. These interactions purchase something valuable, called intimacy. Girls live for intimacy. There are simple rules of balanced exchange girls follow, "buying" or creating intimacy through reliable friendships, a network of relationships, and a sense of belonging.

Girls seek symmetrical connections with one another by talking face-to-face, seeking consensus, negotiating, and carefully avoiding any appearance of superiority. They closely monitor friendships for subtle shifts in alliance and generally prefer to play noncompetitive, turn-taking games like jump rope, house, finger string games, gymnastics, and board games. Girls stridently avoid win or lose situations and can often be observed playing in small, manageable groups or in pairs. Should conflict arise, girls will tend to stop playing. They avoid boasting that creates dislike (except for cases in which they are trying to hurt someone). They express preferences by making suggestions or asking questions.

Girls are relationship machines. They're driven to unify people. Is it any wonder they take marital breakups and dissolution of friendships so hard? It is against their nature to allow these things to happen. Their clear urge is for unity and peace.

Nobody really knows why girls develop this way. It doesn't really matter, though. All that can be reliably ascertained is that for whatever reason, girls around the globe express this predilection for relational symmetry. It is not taught to them, but rather appears to be a natural urge from which they seem unable, and unwilling, to depart.

Bestowing Life

One time not long ago, our family went to get ice cream on a hot summer night. We went to our favorite haunt, a local soft ice cream joint that fixes up your cone any way you like. Our daughter Jessie, in her inimitable fashion, asked the girl at the counter for ice cream with a face on it. The attendant graciously complied, and with an assortment of condiments created a face on the ice cream.

Jessie wouldn't eat the cone. It was "too cute," and she didn't want to hurt it! After some cajoling on our part, the cutesiness wore off and we made her eat the thing! With great hesitation and pity she finally gobbled down her friend, all the while apologizing to the melting face!

Remember, girls are attracted to faces, beginning at birth. This attraction grows over time and reflects what we feel is an important trait of healthy girlness, namely, nurturance. *Nurturance* has a linguistic root meaning "childrearing" and reflects an interesting ability displayed by all girls. When for instance girls play with dolls, the tendency is to give dolls life and make them relatable. They inject life into these empty objects, interact with them, and most likely are learning some of the early lessons of creating symmetrical contact.

Giving life to inanimate objects reflects a common desire among girls to have children. The desire to have children remains a dominant force in girls as they grow and focuses their behavior on caregiving.

Self-Awareness

Girls also have an emerging sense of self-awareness as they develop, and it affects how they see others and how they make choices.

It happens like this: Because of an immature central nervous system, very young girls lack the capability to know the extent to which they are distinct from the world around them. They don't know they exist, they have no consciousness of self. It's only because of a rapidly developing brain that such an awareness becomes possible. Self-awareness occurs in response to a brain that is able to bring such awareness into being.

Self-awareness brings other changes as well. Girls for the first time can take the perspective of others, can begin to see more clearly cause and effect relationships between events, and can begin to see themselves as others might see them. For a period of time spanning through the early teens, an ever-expanding sophistication in thinking exists side-by-side with a familiar and hard-to-relinquish immaturity.

This era, filled with many contradictory yet perfectly normal events, drives parents crazy. Girls during this period are preoccupied with:

How they appear to others
Others' emotional states
Being on the "inside" in relationships
Looks, styles, and attitudes
Maintaining close friendships at any cost

The only solace comes in the fact that the phase eventually passes, leaving girls with the amazing ability to act adultlike and make decisions in new, complex ways, thanks to a new deftness in logic.

These thinking abilities of course lead to a whole rack of new and difficult adjustments in relationships, especially with parents. Girls' thinking will appear flip-floppy as they bounce from thesis to antithesis with ease. They will practice this newfound ability to see both sides of the coin for entertainment as often as for real. They will struggle with how to handle "new" insights emanating from logical deductions of other people and from being able to see things from others' perspective. Parents unaware of this development might mistakenly see their daughters as obstreperous and difficult, when in fact they are being perfectly normal. Over the course of years, though, they settle into sensibility and a consistency that is delightfully complex!

The Big Picture

Thankfully, you needn't have a high level of knowledge in any of these arenas of development to be a highly effective parent. Keep in mind that people weren't meant to have to go to graduate school to raise healthy and progressive girls! It was intended to be done by any of us.

What's important to success is not detailed knowledge of child development; it's not a sophisticated grasp of scientific research or formal rules for raising girls; it is, rather, an understanding that nature courses forward and creates a child capable of tackling life.

What then is required of you? In addition to the list offered in the preceding chapter, you need patience and a sense of balance. The *Girls!* Team assures us that no matter how bizarre this development trail may become, girls pass through it and lean constantly toward the higher ground of feminine maturity and dignity.

Giggles, Glamour, and Glee

Becoming a Girl Again

Movies are the modern method of transmitting folklore within our culture. As with the storytellers of old, through them are passed values, morals, history, knowledge, and entertainment.

One of our favorite movies is *Mrs. Doubtfire.* This is a movie about an estranged father (played by Robin Williams) who dresses like an aging nanny so he can spend time with his kids. His metamorphosis lands him in some difficult spots that nicely highlight the point of this chapter: What must it be like to be a girl? There is a deep gulf of understanding and appreciation between the genders that is difficult to see across.

Men wonder what girlhood must be like but are for the most part unaware of the details. Women try to remember what girlhood was like but often find it difficult. The closest glimpse either of us gets is only a faint, far-off glimmer. However, raising winning girls requires that for just a moment you become one!

How? Well, we have an idea.

The Art-Appreciation Experiment

Our fabulous *Girls!* Team has agreed to help us. Their smiles in reminiscing girlhood suggest that we all might be in for some fun!

How do girls look at the world? Recapturing and capturing girlhood entails learning to experience the world in a different way. Try this old art-appreciation experiment: Find some object and place it in front of you (lampshade, vase, knick-knack, etc.). Close your eyes for about ten seconds, then slowly open them and gaze at the object. As you gaze, imagine that you are an alien looking at that object for the very first time and have never seen anything like it, so all you can do is notice its distinctive features and oddities; notice the contours, colors, shades, size, shape, sounds, feel, smell, or taste of the object. Experience it as if for the first time, and hold the newness as long as you can.

If you're like most students, you can easily gain a new view of something that's existed for years in your life as a "same-old" object. Nothing has changed; you are just suddenly attentive to what has always been there. Old objects become new when you simply change your worn-out view.

This chapter is about giving you that kind of fresh perspective on girls. Think of yourself as a guest visiting a new culture. Let's say that for fun you decided to really taste the local flavor. What would you do? Learning the culture wouldn't be hard, but it would require time and effort. You would need to learn some of its language, sayings, innuendoes, styles, ways, food, folklore and history, games, and jokes. Interestingly, girls have all of these aspects in their culture; learning them transports you to a special world.

A Quick Note to Those
with Disappointing Girlhoods

We're realists and understand that many readers have had rough lives. Don't let that stop you now. Thankfully, life has provided you with some good things to look back on, no matter how compelling the awful things are. We would strongly urge you to take this moment to look over your past and find good memories to build on. In many ways, what you see in your past depends upon how you look at it. You have choices. One choice is to look at the positive aspects of your childhood.

Let's Sail Away!

My (Kathi's) friend Elaine loves to swing. If there's a swing set in the area, she'll be on it. One day we were swinging and having a conversation about her obsession with playground equipment. "I love sailing way up high and feeling the rush of the wind going past," she said with a contagious twinkle in her eye. It made me remember . . .

The playground was a magical place. I spent tireless hours at the playground soaring high on the swing with my pony-tail flying behind me. I felt exhilarated as I pumped my legs harder and harder, certain I could reach out and touch a cloud or perhaps a passing bird. The monkey bars invited me to climb to the tip-top and view the world from the "heavens." Perched atop my pinnacle, the world became small and con-querable. I recall flipping over the bars and dangling upside down, my belly button peeking out. These were magical moments that brought me hours of pleasure. I was thankful Elaine had invited me back to the playground.

As adult women, it's so much fun to relive these moments. It can happen suddenly while chatting with a friend or by spending time with our daughters, living again what they are living for the first time. How about we get back on the swing and sail into our girlhood? Beware, though: You might find yourself getting giggly, lighthearted, and uninhibited in the process. Enjoy it!

Do you remember playing house? My sister Karen and I would gather up all of our plastic dishes, cardboard box

stoves and sinks, and set up our homes. We carefully chose
our families from an odd assortment of dolls, named each
of them, and moved right on in. We chatted to one another
on our pink plastic phones about childrearing problems and
our husbands. Of course the favorite part of playing house
was dressing up in Mom's discarded clothes and jewelry.
And don't forget the high heeled shoes and purse to match!
Once in a while Mom joined in the fun by applying rouge
to our cheeks and bright red lipstick to our tiny kissers.
Though I don't recall ever seeing a woman who even
remotely resembled us, I thought at the time that we were
the image of Mommy!

Do you remember having fits of uncontrollable laughter?
They always seem to happen over the dumbest little things.
For example, our daughter, Jessie, and I occasionally spring
into a spontaneous song. Our sons refer to these as "girl
moments" and are more than happy to leave, fast. On one
occasion we were dancing and singing our own rendition of
the *Sleeping Beauty* theme song:

I know you,
You walked with me once upon a dream;
I know you,
The look in your eyes is so familiar to me . . .

Well, that's the way it's supposed to go. As we went on, our
made-up verses became more and more ridiculous. Finally
Jessie sang:

I know you,
The smell of your socks is so familiar to me . . .

We rolled around holding our stomachs, tears streaming
down our faces, laughing wildly. It was great, and so silly!
For a moment, I was ten again.

From time to time, Jessie whistles that tune as she passes by, and we giggle and wink at each other. I think we created a special moment the two of us will share forever.

And slumber parties! The term itself conjures up thoughts of girls in pink flannel nightgowns huddled close together eating popcorn and brownies in someone's rec room. Remember all the lively discussions about best friends, immature boys, secrets, books, movie stars, clothes, and hair? All the junk food you were forbidden at home was a short hop away in the kitchen. Remember the finger in warm water trick? The girl who stayed up latest was always the envy of the rest. I try to recall those magical nights when my daughter asks me to host such events.

How about special childhood sensations? Remember stepping with bare feet into cool, thick mud and feeling it squirt up between your toes? Dancing in cold rain puddles after a spring shower? Did you ever bury your feet deeply into a sandbox or at a beach? What a marvelous feeling, having that warm sand sifting between each little piggy. Feet were never meant to be stuffed into shoes, unless of course it was your very first pair of shiny black Mary Janes.

I think perhaps we're on a roll. Here is a list of some other common memories. Ponder each, taking time to see, hear, feel, taste, and smell again. Keep the swing moving, and with the innocence of a girl sail back in time!

Jump rope rhymes
Homemade ice cream
Your first pet
Singing in the dark
Painting your fingernails by yourself
Sewing your first outfit
Jealousy when your best friend played with someone else
Misunderstandings
Barbies, and needing just one more outfit
Flowers

Jumping into leaf piles
Diaries
Telling secrets
Your favorite doll
Your best friend
Weird words and sounds
Running as fast as you could just for the feel of it
Cartwheels down hills
Great Halloween costumes
Decorating Christmas cookies
Girls who wore nicer clothes
Playing outside on cool summer nights
Immature boys
Wanting to be noticed or wanting to disappear

Remembering these things can make you feel as if time had swept over you like a warm breeze on a summer night. You'd be a wise woman to keep these feelings for as long as possible. They are brushstrokes of vivid insights for raising winners, all emanating from a better knowledge of yourself!

Fellas, It's Time!

Okay, we can be candid now: This chapter has been the most difficult one for us to write. We started with the assumption that given a willing man and enough coaching he could in time actually feel girlhood. We quickly discovered that capturing girlhood is hard enough once you've been through it, but making it accessible to those who haven't? Well, it's . . . perplexing! All we can do is find roughly similar feelings to those of girls, then try our best to fit those feelings with our individual life experiences. It's worth a try. If at any point you begin feeling too strange and "girly," rest assured that you are accomplishing our objective. Knowing firsthand what those feelings are will make you a terrifically effective (if awkward-feeling) dad.

Think of the whole range of human experience as a big color wheel. You can easily focus on any part of the wheel that you choose, but naturally over time you develop your favorite colors. This, of course, colors the way you see the world. What's interesting is that to some extent we tend to think other people have the same favorite colors we do. Not so. Especially not so with girls.

Girls care about colors on the spectrum of experience that males don't care much about. If men prefer reds, girls prefer blues. If men care about words, girls care about the sounds of words. If men care about objects, girls care about relations between the objects. Girls focus on networks of alliances. Their world is about finding groups of people to which they can belong. Their world is about reading between the lines of what people are saying, carefully watching how they act, and figuring out all the details of what's happening. Though boys can do these things too, let's attempt to find how it feels to be a girl doing them.

We have four simple objectives: (1) to help you experience the unique sensitivity girls have to the world around them; (2) to show how they are driven to connect; (3) to help you experience building rapport through talking and nonverbal attachments to people; and (4) to help you experience what it feels like to have a life-or-death urge to belong and relate.

Sensitivity

Your first lesson requires sensitivity training. Now don't groan! When we say sensitivity training we're referring to your literal ability to sense. Girls are hypersensitive: They sense things happening about them that most men just don't pick up. This is probably the reason women develop such sharp intuitions. They are highly tuned in and can gather and assimilate information about others that men just tend to ignore.

The clearest example of this sensitivity is in the physical realm: Have your daughter scratch your back. Notice how lightly she scratches; it's almost impossible to get her to do it hard enough. She hesitates digging in because of how it would feel to her. She doesn't want to hurt you.

This high sensitivity exists in other areas. She's sensitive to the facial expressions, moods, and voice tones of others. Men must remember this because we tend to have higher thresholds of sensitivity to both physical and interpersonal stimulation. Girls experience the world at a sharper level of intensity.

I (Bill) had a friend in high school named Becky. I was a normal guy and hadn't really spent much time learning the details of relating to girls. As a result, I tended to treat them like guys—not that I was mean to them, I just tended to be brusque, hugging too hard, slapping them on the back too much, talking too loudly, scruffing up their hair. One day Becky had had enough. She took me aside and told me that it was time I learned something about girls: They are sensitive and want to be treated gently.

"Huh? What's 'gentle'?" I huffed.

She was quick to demonstrate. She took my hand and gently placed it on her shoulder. I remember feeling wimpy, like I was touching a rose petal. I couldn't imagine her feeling such a gossamer touch. "I sure couldn't feel that," I lamely grunted to myself.

I was very thickheaded. Becky patiently informed me that I was a Neanderthal but that if I practiced I could improve. I did practice and I did improve. Today Becky lives nearby, and I never give her a hug without thinking about not doing it *too hard!*

You have a very alert and sensitive young woman. Her world is softer than yours, requiring less stimulation to get the same strength of feeling. Listen to the complexity, perhaps even emotionality, of her favorite music. She hears nuances in sound, pitch, and rhythm with remarkable shrewdness. Touch her clothes and shoes; they reflect her acute tactile sensitivity. Her other senses are equally sharp.

The Drive to Connect

Girls are contact beings. This means that they seem constantly driven to unite people and things, to put them together and forge unbreakable alliances. They do this through face-to-face talking and making physical contact with people and objects. Touch is important to girls, and they will fight for it.

We mentioned earlier that little girls have what appears to be a natural attraction to faces. The preference for direct facial contact remains for life, and it seems that people don't become real to girls until they have a face. Eye-to-eye, face-to-face contact creates interdependence that girls lock on to. Facial expressions say to girls that they matter and are acceptable. You have enormous "face value" and can test it for yourself by sitting down with your girl and conversing, always looking directly into her face.

One time I tried this with a little girl in Sunday school. I sat with her for no more than sixty seconds, looking squarely into her face and smiling as we chatted. Then suddenly, inexplicably, she leaped into my arms and hugged me as she laughed. I thought about that odd experience for a long time, and though I'm pretty smart, I still haven't a clue about what that urge must have been like for her. But something very powerful was happening in her.

One of our *Girls!* Team members related a similar story highlighting the agelessness of this need. She told about a woman she knew rather well but with whom she had never had a close, comfortable relationship. After some thought (prompted by this chapter), she concluded the reason for her discomfort: The woman in question had "shifty eyes" and never seemed to laugh much. As long as this woman was just listening to conversation, she could maintain good eye contact. But when she talked, she shifted her posture away, and her eyes "looked like popcorn flying around." This inability to make eye contact prevented a close relationship between these two women.

In addition to a natural urge to connect, girls feel some pressure to fit in. Part of the unspoken culture of girls is that to rise above those you're connected to, or to appear to rise above them, is very bad. Violating this unspoken rule by aggressively seeking status or superiority puts girls at risk of losing valued friendships. Girls like each other to be equal, and seeking status breaks intimacy. Girls want to avoid that.

Something interesting happened not long ago that illustrates this phenomenon. A young girl who lives across the street from us was invited to go to a Yom Kippur celebration with a neighbor. This girl was of Irish descent and was Catholic. As such, Jewish holidays were foreign to her, and she had some questions. We overheard her talking with some other girls about the invitation and were surprised to find out that her biggest fear was whether or not "Jewish people would like a Catholic person." She didn't really seem to care what happened at Yom Kippur, what they would do or say or eat. She just wanted assurances that she'd be accepted and not stick out.

Let's bring this closer to home. What men do—seeking status and superiority over others—is considered by girls to be rude. It is "disconnecting." Whereas men see security and interdependence as weak, girls see them as strengths to be cultivated.

Observe how your daughter reacts to you in two different scenarios. In the first, try to find an interpersonal problem situation in which you can tell your girl that she really needs to "tell so-and-so off"! Focus on encouraging her to be oppositional, just like a guy would, and see how she responds. Then, find a similar situation, but this time rather than being oppositional, be simply warm, fatherly, and supportive. Share experiences you've had that were like hers, tell her you love and stand by her, and touch her gently on the hand—and watch how she responds. If this feels awkward and "girly," then you're doing it right.

Building Rapport

We all know as men what talking means, but let's examine it through the eyes of a little girl. Have you ever felt the desire to just jabber on endlessly? Think about it. Perhaps it's when you're feeling lighthearted at night, perhaps it's when you've been asked about something on which you're an expert, or perhaps it was those premarital marathon conversations you had with your spouse! Do you recall times like these? That is what it's like to be a girl. Talking is effortless and satisfying for them in a way men only glimpse from time to time.

Talking is how girls make things happen. They gain finesse at moving their friends with words and learn in time the particulars of influencing others verbally.

Deborah Tannen, in her book *You Just Don't Understand,* cites a study that noted an interesting trend in how girls talk to one another. She noted that girls tend to speak in long blocks of "matching stories" (sharing similar thoughts, experiences, and feelings). They make strident efforts to draw out each other's thoughts, affirm the other, and empathize with one another, even at very young ages. In this way, girls create rapport that builds long-lasting friendships.[2]

A good way to develop into a girl-like rapport talker is by using "tag questions." Tag questions are those little phrases that act like trailers on the end of the comments we make, like ". . . you know?" or ". . . get what I mean?" or ". . . do you follow?" These questions serve as requests for a response from the listener. Use them, and you are deliberately seeking involvement from the listener.

We mentioned in the last chapter the idea that girls seek symmetry in relationships. Where I went to school there was a girl we called "Canary Terri." She earned that nickname by repeating things other people said. She was just too nice for a bunch of boys to understand. If anything was mentioned, Terri would quickly agree and plunge into her own stories that supported whatever that person just said. She frequently even used the same words as the original speaker's. She was well liked by the other girls, and we boys couldn't understand why.

Girls create symmetry verbally and nonverbally by seeking to match or reflect what someone else is doing rather than trying to "one-up" them or appear in some way better. You can do this with your daughter by using the words "I know what you mean" after she speaks or just before you offer your stories or insights.

Rapport refers not only to this sort of verbal give-and-take but also to nonverbal interaction. Most of us can develop fairly accurate perceptions of others by observing how they walk, their posture, their facial expressions, whether they look us in the eye, and so on. These are the nonverbal telltales girls are so sharp at observing. Is it any wonder they demonstrate such intuitions about people? You can easily heighten your nonverbal rapport with your daughter by simply looking at her, nodding in agreement when she talks, and making physical contact by hugging, holding, and cuddling. These actions can often mean more than a library of perfect words.

A Life-or-Death Urge

A need to belong is the last of those uniquely girl ways of viewing the world that you need to understand. Girls want to be wanted, to matter, to be relevant, to give, and to share a unique place with others.

Here are a few questions to move you a little closer to this intense feeling of belonging that your girl finds quite normal. Have you ever been madly in love, yearning for contact so badly that you call your love immediately after getting home from seeing her? Do you recall that feeling of not being able to get enough? That's how your girl feels about you. Have you ever been intensely homesick, wanting and dreaming about getting back to the place where you are loved and belong? That's how your daughter feels about having your attention.

One of the more revealing discoveries in our work with the *Girls!* Team is how often they mention the importance they placed on their fathers' affirmations. Girls constantly seek affirmations from you, though they little know how to get them. They just do the best they can and hope you'll sense it and deliver. Your affirming her just appears to be one of the determining factors as to whether or not your daughter feels like she belongs.

One night our daughter Jessie decided to act out how she bowed after giving a little speech in class that day. It was dinner time, and the soup du jour was this pasty, gooey French experiment. It looked like it had been troweled out of the back of a cement truck. Jessie stood up on her chair and with regal grandeur closed her eyes and lurched quickly forward . . . headfirst into her bowl! She reared back up suddenly, fifty-weight French glue soup dripping off her nose, only to see me burst out laughing! She responded by bursting into tears.

I felt terrible. She told me later that when she saw me laughing, she thought I was going to make her leave the family! Where she came up with that, I don't know, but I do know that such fear of alienation is foremost in a young girl's mind.

Girls' memories are frequently dominated by experiences with people rather than by events or experiences with things. Whether the subject of their stories is best friends (a hallowed institution among girls) or romance, the preoccupation with relationships seems to focus on anticipation, curiosity, and excitement about people and on enjoying being with others. Your daughter senses value in you as a person, a value that goes beyond material possessions or good times.

Trust is crucial. For boys, trust exists when others are reliable and honest. For girls, trust develops when others value kind words and deeds and offer help, friendship, confidence, and encouragement. Those things cement relationships in place and form what, for lack of better words, are "communities" of girls. It's not a large step to conclude that girls are community builders.

Part **2**

*Building
Extraordinary
Internal Qualities:
Heart,
Mind,
and Spirit*

Growing a Sweet Heart

As he thinketh in his heart, so is he.

Proverbs 23:7 KJV

What Part of You Won't Bend?

A great friend of ours, Mark Montgomery, is a successful motivational and inspirational speaker with profound insight and vision. We were in the audience on one occasion when he challenged listeners to "find in themselves the part that would not bend, no matter what happened"—the part of ourselves that would not melt during moments of intense pressure, the part that would not succumb no matter what the cost, the part that was reliable and firm no matter what travails persisted against it. "Find that part," he challenged, and "you will know the true measure" of yourself.

This notion prompted many conversations. What about us does not bend? Though many of us act at times like social chameleons, there are unwavering parts of us that remain firm under all circumstances. We all have certain unswerving

65

beliefs. What are they? What makes them so strong? Can other beliefs we have be strengthened? Such questions fascinate us, for successfully understanding and building on the unbendable elements in ourselves create a heart of great value.

The set of beliefs, traits, and habits that belong to your daughter make up her character. Character is a concept that's been living a quiet, incognito life in the obscure backwaters of old-fashioned ideas. The root of the word *character* is Greek, meaning "a mark, or distinguishing mark"; used as a verb it means "to make sharp, mark, or engrave." It's a set of unmoving, chiseled-in virtues that don't flex.

Over the last several decades we've scorned inflexibility or stiffness in personality or character. Going with the flow has been more popular. We've generally been more concerned with expedient and practical ways to get along with others and get ahead. The deeper personality traits like trustworthiness and selflessness have been judged too costly and time-consuming. In the short term, we think having character tends to make life impractical and difficult.

Some girls today, however, do know their convictions and won't bend them at all. These girls stand out, usually as leaders. Then there are the girls who know what they believe but routinely bend their convictions to fit in with peers or to just look good. The last group are those girls who never did know what they believe and bend because there is simply no reason not to. When girls have no solid convictions or bend their convictions too easily, they may soon find themselves in difficulty as they discover that the approval of others is fickle.

What is your girl's level of unbendability? Though unbendability varies by age—younger girls tending to be innocently firm and older girls responding to peer pressure—here's the acid test: What beliefs does she hold so firmly that she would gladly suffer public humiliation for them? This is heart—the ability to be true to beliefs in the face of adversity. Anything that is compromised in the face of public pressure or scrutiny is just window dressing. An at-all-costs devotion to basic values defines a girl of genuine heart.

A Most Unlikely Garden

How do we create girls with heart? It used to be thought that heart was inborn. Thankfully for both you and your daughter, that's not true! Anyone can develop devotion to their beliefs. Countless people who don't consider themselves special have exhibited heart in terrible situations. Observing these extraordinary lives has led us to conclude that people are certainly not born with heart but aspire and grow toward it. It's not unlike growing a garden.

You will occasionally read or hear that character is anchored or "determined" by a certain age. You must completely disregard that kind of thinking. Don't be led into thinking your girl is outside any proper age range vital for building qualities of deep character. The young ones can start early, and it's never too late for the older ones. There is always time and there is always a way.

What Does Your Daughter's Garden Grow?

We have been enamored with the following story. It's taken from *Little Men* by Louisa May Alcott and relates a conversation that goes on between an older man, Mr. Bhaer, and a group of small children.

"Once upon a time," began Mr. Bhaer in the dear old-fashioned way, "there was a great and wise gardener who had the largest garden ever seen. A wonderful and lovely place it was, and he watched over it with the greatest skill and care, and raised all manner of excellent and useful things. But weeds would grow even in this fine garden; often the ground was bad and the good seeds sown in it would not spring up. He had many under gardeners to help him. Some did their duty and earned the rich wages he gave them; but others neglected their parts and let them run to waste, which displeased him much. But he was very patient.

"This great gardener gave a dozen or so of little plots to one of his servants, and told him to do his best and see what he could raise. Now this servant was not rich, nor wise, nor very good, but he wanted to help because the gardener had been very kind to him in many ways. So he gladly took the little plots and fell to work. They were all sorts of shapes and sizes, and some were very good soil, some rather stony, and all of them needed much care, for in the rich soil the weeds grew fast, and in the poor soil there were many stones."

"What was growing in them besides the weeds and stones?" asked Nat. . . .

"Flowers," said Mr. Bhaer with a kind look. "Even the roughest, most neglected little bed had a bit of heartsease, or a sprig of mignonette in it. One had roses, sweet peas, and daisies in it"—here he pinched the plump cheek of the little girl leaning on his arm. . . . "As I tell you, some of these beds were easy to cultivate . . . and others were very hard. There was one particularly sunshiny little bed, that might have been full of fruits and vegetables as well as flowers, only it wouldn't take any pains, and when the man sowed, well, we'll say melons in this bed, they came to nothing, because the little bed neglected them. . . . All the bed said was, 'I forgot.'"

Here a general laugh broke out. . . . "I knew he meant us!" cried Demi, clapping his hands. You are the man, and we are the little gardens; aren't we, Uncle Fritz?"

"You have guessed it. Now each of you tell me what crop I shall try to sow in you this spring, so that next autumn I may get a good harvest . . . " said Mr. Bhaer.

"Each of you think what you need most, and tell me, and I will help you to grow it; only, you must do your best, or you will turn out like Tommy's melons—all leaves and no fruit. I will begin with the oldest, and ask the mother what she will have in her plot, for we are all parts of the beautiful garden . . . " said Father Bhaer.[3]

Growing a garden is the right metaphor to describe growing heart in girls.

Three Habits of Green Thumbs

Parents who have grown heart in their girls do three things. Each is something you can easily do too. The first is being a good model. Many of us believe that modeling and being a good model is simply doing some good activity in the vicinity of your child. You assume that your child is watching, that your child is motivated, and that your child understands what you are doing. Such an approach is too passive for a serious gardener of girls. It leaves too much room for misinterpretation.

We've been amazed to discover that what our kids learn from watching us bears no resemblance at all to what we think we're teaching them. One time the kids were having a hard time getting the dog to go outside in the cold. Our dog, Molly, sat defiantly next to the open door, and the kids looked to me for help. Molly is a golden retriever. Most days are bad hair days for this furball! I was dressed for work and didn't want to get gold hair all over me. So I walked up and *gently* placed my toe under her rear and pushed her out the door.

You would have thought I'd cussed! The kids backed away in wide-eyed amazement. "Dad! How can you be so *mean!*" they charged. The accusations continued: "I've never seen you be so rough on a poor defenseless animal!" "Don't you know what that teaches *us* to do, Dad!" "If *I* did that you'd be all over my case," and so on. There I was doing my best to show them how to handle an intransigent dog. And they just thought I was being mean. Where did I go wrong?

I should have modeled from their perspective. This is a powerful way to model that involves notifying your daughter you are going to model something specific (thus getting her attention), doing the modeling, then asking her to recap what she saw you do. It would have been wise for me to say something to this effect: "Kids, if the dog isn't going to go out by our asking her nicely, let's make sure she knows what we mean. Since I'm dressed up, I'm going to do what's easy for me. This won't hurt her a bit . . ." and so on. This simple explanation would have clarified every move I made.

Make it your responsibility to direct your daughter's attention and actively instruct her on what she's seeing. Follow up by clarifying the whole example to be sure you both know what happened.

Second, you need to become skillful in aligning the people in your daughter's life along the same path. Would you plant a prized rose among weeds? Other adults who suggest divisive ideas or are intentionally antagonistic about your daughter's preferences and beliefs are like weeds around your daughter. We adults are skilled at ignoring or avoiding peers who don't line up with what we consider to be good sense and judgment. Little girls, however, are the opposite. They tend to believe what they are told by adults and can become easily mired in confusion.

We realize of course that perfect alignment of all the adults in your girl's world is impossible. However, you must be the one person in her life who champions the effort at alignment. To the best of your ability tell the other adult members in her life what qualities of heart you value and how they can help. The *Girls!* Team unanimously endorses the idea of building a "community expectation" among all her significant adults. This sort of specific group unity is a powerful means by which to influence her behavior. Become active in discussing with your daughter what she's hearing from other adults and what she's thinking about it. In as many ways as are practical, be active in monitoring the input your daughter is receiving. Don't ever be afraid to heighten her access to people (adults or otherwise) who reinforce the attitudes and opinions she needs to hear.

Under the best circumstances, this arranging can be vital to your daughter. Primarily it suggests to your daughter that others in her world are going to be helping her along. Group participation creates not only an expectation of performance, but also a sense that her life is a community project, that she is inside the web of care and help. Such a web fits hand-in-glove with her natural way of viewing the world in terms of communities.

Third, you must learn how to observe and reward small behavior change and patiently build it over time. The gardener needs to know exactly what's been planted and keep a vigil when nothing appears to be happening. Too many of us, after reading a motivational book such as this, want to press the accelerator all the way to the floor and make changes as rapidly as possible. The changes and developments in your child happen in a sluggish fashion—long periods of dormancy punctuated by stuttered bursts of obvious change. Content yourself with not seeing the fruit of your labor for some time. It grows slowly.

Heartsease, Mignonettes, and Daisies

If a girl has heart—clings relentlessly to simple principles—what sorts of flowers would grow in her life? The following would make any heart gardener proud:

- Boldness and courage
- Joy
- Initiative
- Giving herself with love and compassion
- Forgiveness
- Trustworthiness
- Tenacity
- Wisdom

These are phenomenal qualities! They are like flowers, which when arranged together form a bouquet called heart. And they're within reach of your girl! Think of them as seeds to plant. Take the perspective of a patient, confident gardener who spends time thinking about how he or she wants to arrange the seeds in plots to give the most beautiful arrangement in months ahead. Be filled with anticipation and hope as you begin to cultivate the most important garden of your life.

As we introduce each of these qualities and speak of them specifically, we ask that you actively think about the exact place and time of day you can plant each one *today*. Your effectiveness doesn't become dynamic until your action becomes specific.

We will provide examples for you to linger over, but you must create your own way to apply these examples. That's called "owning the material" and is key to being confident and effective. What you simply read you will forget, but what you create for yourself you anchor in a unique way that nobody can snatch.

The stories that follow demonstrate how the seeds that were planted in each of these women's lives have matured and blossomed. Read each and think about how you can model the qualities, align key adults to reinforce them, and begin today to reward their appearance in your girl's life.

Boldness and Courage

There is a woman named Agnes Gonxha Bejaxhiu, Yugoslavian by birth and now a citizen of India. She went to India as an educated eighteen-year-old girl aspiring to join the Sisters of Our Lady of Loretto convent, teaching in their elite school in Calcutta. She taught there until the age of thirty-six, rising to principal and commanding great respect for her talent.

Then one day all things changed. She heard God call her to care for the sick and dying right outside the walls of her private, quiet enclave, so she ventured out into the teeming, squalid slums and never came back. Facing extreme odds, she succeeded in her unique mission and became known to the world as Mother Teresa.

She's well known for doing the impossible by means of simple, innocent boldness. Once, on the approach of the twenty-fifth anniversary of the order she created (Missionaries of Charity), she decided that "her people"—the poor and destitute—should have a humble gift. She decided she could convince a cinema house to air *Ben Hur* free for the lepers and outcasts of the community. It was pure Mother Teresa—thinking up the near impossible, then setting about to do it with no thought of failure. This was her boldness and courage: flying forward on wings of determination when everyone else said, "Land," with never even the slightest consideration of quitting.

Mother Teresa is equally fearsome in the face of opposition, of which she has had plenty. Tell your daughter this story. She once faced an enormous crowd angered by her ongoing care for lepers in a neighborhood slum home. (It was customary to remove lepers to isolated colonies.) Spying a priest from a nearby Hindu temple who was dying of cholera in the street, she quietly walked into the midst of the stone-throwing crowd, picked him up, and carried him back into the house. The taunts and jeers of the terrible mob never ceased, but neither did she.

There are stories of her relentless courage as she mercifully cut off lepers' fingers, created food and supplies out of waste and garbage, and cared for the dying. She did it all in a hostile environment. Her stubborn will and devotion to simplicity have allowed her order to serve "her people" in places ranging from the Australian Outback to Harlem. This is a life worth examining.[4]

Joy

Here's an indispensable quality of heart. We read once that "life is multiplication; if you're a zero inside, you can multiply it by any good thing happening in your life and still end up having a life equaling zero." Don't let your girl be a zero!

We know some zero girls, and to be candid, they're miserable. Thankfully, we know some powers-of-ten girls, too! Those are the ones who leap with fifty thousand watts of joy and love life with boundless energy! They sing, dance, laugh, hug, scream, and click their heels. We like to have those girls around, for they are the quintessential meaning of what it is to really live. And it's contagious.

How do we build this sort of joy? It's easier than you might imagine. Certainly there must be some level of liveliness in your daughter; but that level is present in 99 percent of all girls and just needs some encouragement. We would suggest a specific angle: Teach your daughter that joy is rooted in thankfulness and self-sacrifice. Encourage her to taste and enjoy the world all about her, giving thanks often. Let her feel the joy of making others feel special. Turn ordinary events into special occasions. Make her special, and delight with her as she experiences the world.

Like faith, joy without action is dead. Girls built heart-rich with joy actively shower goodness and excellence throughout the places they occupy. Continually encourage your daughter to give her inner joy to home, school, church, grocery stores, or any other place needing it. Teach her to do it incessantly. The use-it-or-lose-it theme applies here.

Who would embody such joy if not Joni Eareckson Tada? If you don't know this rare woman, we'll let her introduce herself:

> Today as I write these words marks the seventeenth anniversary of that hot summer day when I broke my neck—and altered the whole course of my life. I was seventeen on that day when I dove into the shallow waters of the Chesapeake, so I've now spent as many years in a wheelchair as on my feet. It's been a long journey . . . yes, and a difficult one.
>
> Yet seventeen years have given me plenty of time to adjust and cope. I've even come to the point where I can give thanks. I don't allow myself to live in the past—daydreaming or fantasizing about what might have been. But that's not to say I don't enjoy a good memory now and then. Nice memories have a way of buoying my spirits—especially when I'm feeling frustrated with limitations in general and wheelchairs in particular.
>
> I treasure some of those memories, like the sensation of walking on the warm concrete apron of a swimming pool . . . snapping flowers off their stems with my fingers . . . scouring a sink with sponge and cleanser . . . creaming my own hands . . . brushing a horse's coat . . . or even drumming my fingers on a desk. . . . Those might not sound like much to you, but to me they represent warm sunlit moments from the past . . . parts of life that are warm and sweet and worth remembering.

So on this seventeenth anniversary of my injury I say, *thank-you, God for the wonderful things I can still remember. Thank-you that these memories help me to appreciate how precious our health really is. Oh, and help me, Lord not to take for granted those things I still can feel and do and experience. So many things. And Father . . . may the next seventeen years be as rewarding and enriching as what I've experienced so far.*[5]

Initiative

Initiative is one of life's all-star freedoms. Personal initiative is simply getting up off your duff and taking direct action. It allows you to jump out of feelings of powerlessness, enabling you to take charge of your life. It gives confidence and momentum and eliminates depression and anxiety. And we probably all realize this is true and wish we had more!

Thankfully, initiative is common in girls. It starts with activity, which by now you've noticed is pretty normal for girls. There is no ceiling to their energy level. But a girl's energy and activity tend to be scattered. Focusing her natural activity on something specific and then getting out of the way is how you plant the seeds of initiative. It's like a formula: Energy + direction = initiative. Time spent encouraging natural activity in a specific direction yields a zesty crop of initiative.

Take the story of Sadie and Bessie Delany as an example of what this sort of initiative can accomplish. These two unusual sisters gained national recognition in 1991 when the *New York Times* ran an extensive article celebrating and chronicling their one hundred years of life. They are the only surviving members of one of the nation's most prominent African American families. This family rose to distinction just one generation after the Civil War, and all ten children attended college in an era when few Americans, black or white, ever went beyond high school. They both graduated from Columbia University. Sadie received a teaching degree and taught in the New York City public schools. Bessie earned a dental degree and became the second black woman licensed to practice dentistry in New York.

Imagine the initiative required for such a climb! Their story is replete with one example of racism and sexism after another. But by sheer energy and focus they accomplished what they wanted. They succeeded in a way most of us only read about.

Bessie tells of a particularly memorable event that shows the kind of initiative she had and we need:

> There are plenty of white folks who say "Why haven't negroes gotten further than they have?" They say about negroes, "What's wrong with them?" To those white people I have this to say: "*Are you kidding?*"
>
> Let me tell you something. Even on my graduation day at Columbia I ran into prejudice. It was on the sixth of June, 1923. There I was, getting my Doctor of Dental Surgery Degree, and I was on top of the world. But you know what? The class selected me as the marshall, and I thought it was an honor. And then I found out—I heard them talking—it was because nobody wanted to march beside me in front of their parents. It was a way to get rid of me. The class marshall carried the flag and marched out front, alone.
>
> I don't know how I got through that place [Columbia University] except when I was young nothing could hold me back. No, Sir! I thought I could change the world. It took me a hundred years to figure out I can't change the world. I can only change Bessie. And, honey, that ain't easy, either.[6]

Teach initiative by helping your girl recognize her own strengths and talents. Help her practice expressing her own ideas. Take time to help her set attainable goals and show her how to methodically pursue them. If you teach your daughter to have confidence in her abilities and her ideas, you arm her with the terrific tool of initiative.

Giving Herself with Love and Compassion

Giving generously of oneself remains one of the purest ways to achieve happiness and a true, deep sense of satisfaction. We need to somehow plant that seed.

Most of you have felt that deep satisfaction of knowing you gave of yourself with love and compassion even if you weren't recognized for doing so. Lecturing your girl about that effect will likely go nowhere. These seeds are most easily planted through modeling and practice. Do some of these things with your daughter for no reason other than love and compassion:

Take someone flowers
Deliver a meal to a shut-in
Send a cute card to a teacher or friend
Compliment someone
Respond to someone's obvious needs
Make yourself intentionally uncomfortable in order to
    make someone else comfortable
Share something with someone
Do something nice for a family member without being
    asked

We recently heard a touching story of love and compassion in action. Sixteen-year-old April Fleming was dying of an incurable disease. Just a few weeks prior to her death, the Make-A-Wish Foundation (devoted to making final wishes of dying children come true) approached her about what she would want as a final wish. To their surprise, April asked that they give Christmas presents to homeless children. The foundation administrators were shocked. Such a selfless and compassionate request had never been made. They granted her wish: twelve homeless children in the Seattle area received Christmas gifts, thanks to a lot of love from a very big person.

Another way to plant the seed of giving herself with love and compassion is by helping your daughter bring out the best in others. "How in the world do we teach that?" you might ask. Encourage her to *give to others what they need*. If she becomes deft at reading between the lines of what people say and do, she will quickly notice that most people need things they don't ask for.

Teach her to pay uncommon attention. Show her how to give what her good sense tells her others need. For example, give an encouraging word to someone who looks sad but insists that everything is fine. Give food to someone who obviously has little or none. The opportunities are ample for meeting the needs of others who aren't asking for help.

Probe her opinions and insights, and ask her to suggest ideas about what others might be thinking that they aren't verbally sharing. Strategize as a duo about how certain people might be approached, and in the most practical sense become one in mind and spirit on the best course of advice and action.

Sharing in these ways allows your daughter to experience the process of giving. The power of simple encouragement, which you demonstrate, can have far-reaching influence on her. Encouraged often and simply, these seeds will sprout little buds.

Forgiveness

Forgiveness is one of the most unnatural things an adult human being can do. If it's unnatural for us, you can bet it's perfectly alien to little girls! The reason is that up to the age of nine or ten, girls have difficulty thinking two contradictory things about one person at the same time. Life is black and white: Either you're a good person or a bad person. No in-betweens. This psychological fact challenges our efforts to plant the seeds of two different kinds of forgiveness. But we can meet the challenge.

Seeding the first kind of forgiveness (let's call it "regular" forgiveness) in your girl is hampered because it looks to her as though the guilty person is being let off the hook. This doesn't compute to little girls. Can't you just hear them say, "That's not *fair*!"? Inside a childish mind, the only reply to a wrong is another wrong; it's only fair. It's a complicated adult mental ability to understand that people can be wrong yet forgiven, released from retaliation yet still responsible for what they did. Is it any wonder girls need to be helped to see this?

"Regular" forgiveness has a saintly sister. Her name is "unconditional" forgiveness. Many confounding truths swirl around this unusual kind of forgiveness. Forgive without condition? Inhuman! Impossible! It's human to eventually forgive others, but not before exacting talonsful of flesh. To grow this second sprout and learn to forgive for no reason is quite ungirllike!

This forgiveness reminds us of a Corrie ten Boom story. During World War II, the Nazis entered her native country of Holland and began ordering Jews to the concentration camps. Corrie, her father, and sister all began the honorable but lethal practice of hiding Jews. Unfortunately, the SS caught wind of their activity and promptly sent them to the camps.

There, Corrie's sister and father both died. By what can only be described as a miracle, she survived the brutality and evil of that place and went on after the war to establish rehabilitation centers for former prisoners. As part of her work, she began speaking to large groups about her experiences.

During one such engagement, she had the horrifying surprise of coming face-to-face with her former prison guard. She was surprised to find herself filled with anger, terrible thoughts, and vicious memories. After the speech, the man came forward and attempted to shake her hand and thank her for the message. Since no condition could possibly equate her loss, she had to choose whether or not to unconditionally forgive her ex-tormentor:

> I tried to smile, I struggled to raise my hand. I could not. I felt nothing, not the slightest spark of warmth or charity. And so again I breathed a silent prayer. Jesus, I cannot forgive him. Give me your forgiveness.
>
> As I took his hand, the most incredible thing happened. From my shoulder, along my arm and through my hand a

current seemed to pass from me to him, while into my heart sprang a love for this stranger that almost overwhelmed me.[7]

The abilities to forgive and unconditionally forgive need to be called up out of your daughter. We all have reserves of forgiveness available to us, yet until someone (preferably you) stands on the higher cliff of life and calls your daughter to this higher standard of behavior, she will never know it's possible! You must be like the flashing sign that both informs and alerts your girl to the presence of a situation in which she can exercise forgiveness without condition. Be a gentle, firm reminder that will not be dimmed.

Sometimes the greatest impact you can have in this area is when your daughter is being eaten alive by anger and bitterness. These moments will come and go frequently in girlhood, lasting for only short bursts. Anger and bitterness are easy to spy if you look, so prepare to pounce quickly! Forgiving those who've hurt us extinguishes the bitterness and hatred that can grow quickly out of control, robbing us of happiness and self-control.

Our pastor, Larry Evans, once remarked that when you forgive someone, you put yourself in the position of initiative. Remember initiative? Take some initiative here. Quickly encourage your girl to forgive others without condition. Encourage her to boldly forgive and think nothing more of it.

Forgiveness, like other seeds, is planted through demonstration. It's most effective to go out of your way to forgive others in your daughter's presence. Arrange those situations if you must! Let her see you actively forgiving another person in spite of his or her faults or wrongdoing. She'll be a firsthand eyewitness to godliness in action! What a memorable event on which to lay a foundation for excellence. One or two of those incidents will do more to move your daughter in the direction of heart than a year's worth of seminars or a truckload of childrearing videos.

Another uncluttered view to forgiveness is provided when you ask your daughter's forgiveness. We all commit atrocious errors with our girls, so although it's tough, go to her in a quiet moment and ask forgiveness. It's a bonding event. Never underestimate the power that asking forgiveness has to plant a good seed.

Trustworthiness

Like all the other flowers, trustworthiness develops over time. The generally accepted requirements for trustworthiness are:

Truthfulness
Consistency
Integrity
Being forthright and forthcoming
Submitting to authority

If we are all honest with ourselves, we'll admit that adhering to this list is tough. What then should we expect from our girls? We should expect that our girls will follow the "monkey see, monkey do" rule. You are the head monkey and you define your girl's uppermost level of trustworthiness. Your successes and failures in this arena are magnified, and your girl is watching, so you must put yourself on alert. Be the model of trustworthiness. You cannot lead your girl anywhere you yourself cannot go.

Tenacity

In my Raising Winners seminar I often repeat that the world wants your daughter out of the way. The world wants your daughter to quit, to go home and watch T.V. In Dante's poetic tale *The Inferno*, we read that the inscription on the gate to hell reads, "Abandon Hope All Ye Who Enter Here." That sign might just as well hang on the walls of maternity rooms, for from birth, the predicaments of life seem intent on stealing our hope.

Some people fight back. Some people take their lives back. We want to encourage you to have one of those daughters willing to take her hope back! Remind her that struggle is part of growing up, and all she needs to do is keep moving on. Be her optimism! Be her voice that says, "Don't quit!"

So many extraordinary examples of tenacity fill our minds, but a recent example of two ordinary, tenacious women is particularly memorable. Their names are Winson and Dovie Hudson. They live in a place that was once rife with Ku Klux Klan activity. The African American people of the town were terrified by continual harassment and intimidation, but they stood up to it. Winson says:

> My dad was brave. He had that hostility in him 'cause they hung his brother. When the Ku Klux Klans would come through here, other people would come to our house for safety. My daddy was not afraid, and that taught us. We never was afraid of them. . . . The more they did to us, the meaner we got.[8]

To this very day, Winson and Dovie fight forward. They don't know what it is to quit. They can't quit. They've been instrumental in desegregation efforts in the schools, democratizing voter registration for blacks, establishing preschool centers, and implementing nutrition programs for children—all within an environment that would make most of us wither and fold.

Girls must learn to push themselves, for by nature they quit when discomfort or fear comes upon them. Sow the seeds of tenacity early.

Wisdom

Throughout life we gain an ever-increasing understanding of right and wrong, healthy and unhealthy, good and evil.

Knowing which is which is wisdom. Gaining wisdom is a life-long pursuit requiring practice and mastered only by trial and error. The best place to help your daughter begin her pursuit of wisdom may surprise you. Encourage her to be fearlessly honest with herself.

The road to wisdom begins with radical self-honesty. Like all of us adults, she'll try to excuse herself and blame others for her weaknesses and mistakes. Refuse to buy into it. Gently lead her to be honest with herself. This creates a person of both humility and wisdom.

Encourage your daughter to:

Identify people (usually adults) whom she considers wise to ask for advice

Admit and claim weaknesses and develop alliances with others to strengthen herself

Talk about both the good and not-so-good qualities of her friends

Admit that there may be a better way to handle problems or to behave

Discuss what that better way might be

We have in our kitchen a jar filled with proverbs written on small pieces of paper. It's called the Wisdom Jar. We often grab that jar at dinner, choose one of the proverbs, and read it aloud. The encouragement or insight is always fresh and timely. The kids often perk up and tell of an incident *that day* related to what is on the piece of paper. Discussions begin and wisdom grows. Fertilize your girl's little heart with good sense, stimulation, and direction.

Her Part

Do these things and in time you'll see hints of a blossoming heart. All that's required of your girl is watchfulness, listening, and obedience to your words.

We'll grant you that these requirements sound out of place these days. We are strong advocates of parents taking control of their homes and as much as possible defining how children will act, expecting that behavior without question. Take charge! Few qualities of heart will evolve without some parental involvement. In other words, your daughter will loaf off in the most thoughtless way if given the option.

If there's a trick to this it's helping her to have heart for her own good reasons, not because you demand it. That internal structure takes time to cultivate, requiring you to be an active and attractive model, and requiring her to mature. Just maintain your faith and confidence, and the time will come when the garden will bloom.

We also strongly recommend that for her part, your daughter familiarize herself with great heroines like those we've mentioned in this chapter. There are many women who are great models. Ask your girl to read those stories, listen to them on audio or videotape, and find for herself other models—women she respects and admires. She will of course do this anyway, but you should be careful not to underestimate the power you have to introduce her to remarkable people.

My Girl's So Bright
I Gotta Wear Shades

It is not enough to have a good mind. The main thing
is to use it well.

René Descartes

The child is endowed with unknown powers, which can
guide us to a radiant future. If what we really want is a
new world, then education must take as its aim the
development of these hidden possibilities.

Maria Montessori

I (Bill) once asked a little girl in our neighborhood if she
knew who Einstein was.

"Oh yeah, he's the guy who put bubbles in beer!" she
blurted.

"No, I think not!" I chortled.

"Oh yes he did, Mr. Beausay! I saw it in a movie. He went
out into his dad's shed and used a chisel to split a Tasmanian

85

beer atom, and when he finally crunched it, the shed blew up, and his mug of beer got full of bubbles. I know; I saw it!"

"Honey, . . . um, what was the name of this movie?" I asked.

"*Young Einstein*. It's all about his life growing up in Tasmania, starring Yahoo Serious." Hmmph! Aced once again by this pesky movie business! (Not only is this a true story, but such a movie exists too!)

Your daughter's brain is a fantastic creation. It's always attempting to make sense of our world. What excites us most is that understanding cognitive development is remarkably easy. Influencing it is easy too. Your daughter can easily gather information more quickly than she does now, apply simple logic, improve her memory, and achieve greater academic success than her current level. What may be most important is that she can become more comfortable with her brain and eventually use it in creative, flexible, and independent ways.

The sprawling galaxy of books about creating the "softer" side of our daughters (emotions, self-esteem, and so on) has blinded us to the importance of building her best asset, her brain. The results of trying to build thinking ability are uniformly positive.

Diamonds Are a Girl's Best Friend

If building a mind has a good analogy, it's diamond cutting. Let's start in the diamond field. You would not know this place from any other rock-strewn field you've ever seen. You could easily step on hundreds of diamonds and not even recognize them, because in rough form, they look just like rocks. They're made of simple carbon arranged in a cubic structure and squished together with unthinkable pressure over thousands of years (diamonds often explode when being mined because of the terrific tension in their chemical architecture).

In the hands of a skilled diamond cutter, these drab pebbles reveal an alluring fire. Carefully measuring the right proportions and exact angles, the cutters put facets, or faces, on the stones, allowing them to reflect and refract light with magnificent brilliance, clarity, and color. Keep in mind that it's only when faceted that ordinary "diamonds in the rough" acquire the distinctive sparkle and character that make each unique.

Our girls' brains are like diamonds. They're built by a combination of simple elements, pressed over time, with the proper facets cut for brilliance, clarity, and color. We as parents facilitate the whole diamond-cutting process. We help build the real thinking ability our daughters will carry with them to adulthood. How? you might ask. It all starts in the atmosphere you create.

You Are the Diamond Cutter

There is a certain atmosphere created when parents make a willful decision to help a girl develop a good brain. The task of creating the right kind of pressure to do this job is yours. The responsibility to respond is your daughter's.

Oprah Winfrey grew up in a diamond-cutter's atmosphere, and as a result she's grown to have a radiance we all see. "I was raised to believe that excellence is the best deterrent to racism and sexism, and that's how I operate my life," she says. In her case, and in the case of others who have grown to prominence, pressure to perform was applied early. By the age of seven her grandmother required her to read five books every two weeks, and she had vocabulary lists to learn. "I believe that education is power," she says. She'd be the first to recommend this demanding atmosphere to parents interested in creating positive growth inside their daughter's head.

No Brains Required

Before we begin a thorough explanation of how to sculpt thinking ability into our girls, it's wise to discuss a subtle problem. Though times are evolving, American families still lack a commitment to education. There seems to be a widely believed, misguided idea that it's the solitary responsibility of the schools to educate. Not true! Schools can only support and embellish whatever education goes on in the home. Education is a homebound activity first that schools support.

Parents must exhibit a fondness of learning and teach their children to be curious information seekers. Thankfully, learning is a natural, whole-life activity. Maria Montessori said:

> We know how to find pearls in the shells of oysters, gold in the mountains, and coal in the bowels of the earth, but we are unaware of the spiritual germs, the creative nebulae that the child hides in himself when he enters the world.[9]

Let's acknowledge the hidden potential of your child. The educational establishment is trying to harvest this talent. They are currently trying all means possible to involve parents in the day-in, day-out job of stimulating children at home. We can do our part by making our homes places where education has priority.

Recognize that when you apply low-pressure, long-term demands for specific behavior—like thinking—girls respond with action—like thinking. It's as if they are designed to adapt to whatever is demanded of them. We must simply make a habit of asking of our girl what we want, especially when it comes to stretching her ability to think.

Back when I was a professional therapist, I worked with many children. I recall one little girl, age ten, who had what her mother called a "motivation problem." This little girl had no apparent interests, no close friends, no hobbies, and as nearly as I could tell, no life at all. She would come home from school and retreat to her room to simply fiddle-faddle the evening away. Her mother didn't know how to respond to this, so she continued expecting little in order to avoid any "damaging stress" for the girl.

Well, at the time I was a therapist who believed you could get kids to do almost anything (I still believe it). I didn't think this girl was depressed; she hadn't had any trauma, and none of the classic telltales lined up. Yet she slipped further and further into obscurity and isolation. Obscurity was easy, as it turned out, because she had no requirements to meet.

The real challenge in this case was getting her parents to press their pampered little hermit just a bit. I explained to them that within normal families, members try to develop cognitively, emotionally, and spiritually to fit into what is expected of them. If there is a need for some specific trait or behavior, family members, regardless of age, will create it in some way.

I strongly suggested that their first move should be to demand more of her and let her natural adaptiveness respond. We started with excruciatingly simple things like making her decide what she would wear to school, making her fix her own cereal, getting her to carry her own books. These are small matters, but for a girl living in a world void of expectations, this list was an ever-so-slight stretch.

This girl began to bloom. After the initial outrage of no longer having Mom and Dad waiting on her, she quickly perked up and did with little fuss all those things she was asked to do. It's been my experience that far from expecting too much of our kids, we tend to expect not nearly enough of them. Kids like to excel. Kids like to feel some control of their lives and need parents to help them develop their abilities. They enjoy being pushed to excel if they know you're in it with them.

Seven Rough Cuts

Even the most exquisite diamonds begin with rough cuts, are perfected with finer cuts, and are finally polished. Every little girl is born with seven rough cuts, or facets, of intellect. Long ago it was thought intelligence was a one-dimensional, logical-mathematical ability. That idea is extinct. Dr. Howard Gardner, Harvard psychologist and researcher, has demonstrated that we all have at least seven different types of intelligences. These intelligences coexist inside each person's head, independent of one another and in different proportions.

It's as if our heads were great big watermelons divided into seven unequal pieces that fit together perfectly like a juicy puzzle. We each have all seven pieces, but the shapes and sizes of the seven chunks are all different.

The seven intelligences, in no particular order, are:

1. Linguistic intelligence
2. Logical-mathematical intelligence
3. Spatial intelligence
4. Musical intelligence
5. Bodily-kinesthetic intelligence
6. Interpersonal intelligence
7. Intrapersonal intelligence

Linguistic intelligence has to do with one's ability to use words. Those endowed with large watermelon pieces of this intelligence are the writers, poets, storytellers, attorneys, and politicians. These people tend to speak well and enjoy words and reading.

Logical-mathematical intelligence is the piece of intelligence most often associated with brainy people: scientists, accountants, computer wizards, and so on. These individuals have a naturally large slice of sequence thinking, logic, reason, and rationality.

Those individuals with big pieces of *spatial intelligence* have the gift of thinking in pictures and images. They have an acute sensitivity to visual images and as such tend to be the artists, photographers, mechanical engineers, and designers of the world.

Musical intelligence should be easy to figure out. Those with large-scale musical intelligence can create melodies, find rhythm and tone, and easily discern different types of music.

Bodily-kinesthetic intelligence is the intelligence of the athletes and others with great physical skill, such as craftsmen and surgeons. Their unique gift is controlling and manipulating themselves and objects in their world with precise movements.

Interpersonal intelligence is being able to work well with others and understand them. These people have exceptional capacity to perceive the moods and temperaments, intentions and desires of others. They seem to have an uncanny ability to get into the heads of others and accurately discern motives and feelings.

Intrapersonal intelligence is being able to understand one's inner self. These people are good at introspection and self-examination. They excel in discriminating between their own different emotional states. People gifted in this way are the counselors, theologians, and business leaders.

Everyone has each of these seven intelligences. We're certain that as you read through the list you found yourself thinking about your own ability and which of the seven intelligences you have in greatest potency. That's normal. Now we want you to think about your girl and begin to think which intelligences she has in greatest strength.

You can do her a further favor and publicly recognize her greatest intelligence, and let her know you think she's smart! Ask her to demonstrate it! Seeing which intelligence is her strongest precipitates her self-confidence. Everyone is smart in his or her own way, and anybody, with reasonable self-discipline and drive, can gain good mastery over any of these intelligences. The great thing about this conception of intelligence is that it's all-inclusive; everybody can find at least one reason to look in the mirror and conclude, "I've got brains!"

Press On!

This seven-piece view of intelligence is more and more finding root in our school systems. The effect is mixed. It's a blessing because all students can feel as though they're intelligent. It's a curse because many kids on discovering they're "adequate" simply quit pushing themselves in their weak areas. They don't yearn for greater things, and if let off the hook don't expect much of themselves. They refuse to stretch themselves.

Allow us to make a radical statement: Minds need to be stretched in systematic ways. We must stop incessant praising for shoddy thinking and weak academic performance. Praise without performance is a delusion. Like a diamond cutter, we need to set and maintain high standards. It would be wonderful if excellence were easy, but it just isn't. Excellence is earned. Accomplished girls are made. Our girls need to be made comfortable with stretching their inborn gifts and honing and polishing the natural fire and allure God designed into them.

Einstein was once lecturing about the nature of the universe, explaining its terrific simplicity. "What if you find out that the world isn't so simple and is in fact complex?" questioned a student.

"Then I wouldn't be interested in it anymore," he replied. "God wouldn't miss the chance to make the universe this simple." Let's commit ourselves to simplicity in stretching the intelligences of our girls.

Our approach is straightforward. We wish to focus on three skills that stretch all seven intelligences:

- Reading and remembering information
- Active thinking and learning
- Ordering and sequencing your thinking

Help your girl master these three skills and her seven inborn intelligences will flourish.

Reading and Remembering

We were all born and raised to live in a world that no longer exists. Information overload is now a common social fever.

It's been said that more news is contained in one Sunday issue of the *New York Times* than a person a hundred years ago was exposed to in an entire lifetime! What's being done to help our children deal with this blitz is whatever *you're* doing. Most girls are left on their own to find ways to handle the maelstrom. And most of them are tuning out.

We have a better idea. Teach your girl how to walk on the information wave by reading more effectively and improving her memory. Reading is the easiest and perhaps most efficient tool to use to sort through volumes of information.

The Week of the Big, Friendly Giant

The kids and I (Kathi) recently spent a week with a big, friendly giant. He came to our house at about sundown on several consecutive nights to escort us on an unusual journey. We secretly snickered about his huge teeth that reminded us of slices of white bread, and we eventually got accustomed to his huge ears that seemed as big as truck wheels as they flapped and twisted on his head. He taught us new words we'd never heard, like *frobscottle* and *whizzpopper,* and introduced us to other, not-so-friendly giants, like Fleshlumpeater and Gizzardgulper.

Our friend was alive to us for days, and he made us laugh and cry, shiver and jump. We helped him carry out an important mission. Then at the end of several nights' journey, we bid our giant friend farewell. It closed the book on an epic adventure, leaving us with much more than just fond memories. As a family we were touched by a warmth and glow that lingers even now.

Our Big Friendly Giant (BFG) popped off the pages of the well-known Roald Dahl book of the same title. Can't you just picture us there snuggled together each night anxious to hear how our heroine Sophie and the wordsmithing BFG were going to fix their gigantic and perplexing problems? Though we are hard-pressed to explain it in depth, something magical happened as we listened, imagined, and laughed together at the exploits and silliness of our imaginary friend. Words are so very powerful.

Beyond the warmth and coziness, education was happening. Through the medium of a story read aloud, the kids were learning in the most traditional way about language and the use of verbal abilities.

We all know reading is important to kids, but perhaps nobody ever explained why. It goes beyond merely learning language. Consider these reasons:

1. Books are filled with a rich variety of vocabulary and descriptive phrases. Hearing those words in proper context, especially within a story, broadens your daughter's knowledge base and ability to express herself in new ways.

2. Grammar rules, which many experts think are the earliest building blocks of logic, are introduced and reinforced within the confines of a story.

3. Stories provide the opportunity to think and synthesize, predict outcomes, discuss cause and effect, and recognize common idioms in the reader's native language. All of these higher-level reasoning skills are vital in developing thinking. A member of the *Girls!* Team told a funny story about one of her daughters recovering from a sickness. This little one wished to go outside, but her mother said she wasn't so sure. The little girl disappeared, only to return moments later with Dr. Spock's book on baby and child care and the suggestion that Mom look up whether or not it was all right for her to go outside!

4. Kids who read well move ahead faster in life. Literacy is the key to educational achievement.

5. It's fun! This may be the best reason of all to read. Choose books of intrigue or mystery for your girl. Find books rich in images of fanciful characters and far-off

places. Your library is filled with adventures waiting to be discovered.

Educators understand the vital role language plays in the development of your girl. Teachers also realize that grammar rules, spelling, and vocabulary skills learned in isolation from one another is an inefficient way to learn. In response, educators have created an approach to teaching you'll be seeing more of in coming years. It's called "whole language" and greatly enhances the process of education by integrating each element of the school curriculum into one theme.

For example, teachers select one theme or topic and use it as the foundation of all subject areas. Let's say for instance that the selected theme is Native American Indians. For social studies, students might learn about tribal cultures and their locations around the continental U. S. For science they might study the weather and how the Native Americans adapted to it. The health portion might cover the foods Native Americans consumed and whether they were healthy or not. Reading might include stories about Native Americans or fictionalized accounts of historic moments involving Native Americans. Math would be taught by counting tribes, studying barter systems, or using Native American examples in solving various mathematical problems. The writing lesson could be to compare the students' daily life with that of various tribes. Teachers like the Whole Language system because when it works well, children become active participants in their own education.

The Whole Language method can be tailored for home use. Familiarize yourself with the subjects being taught at school, then simply join in by using resources you have at home. We heard of a case in which a girl was studying about Aztec ruins. Wishing to further promote this exploration, Mom and Dad encouraged her to find where the ruins would be on a map and call the airlines to find out what it would cost to travel to them. Though the parents had no intention of actually making the trip, they used the inertia and focus of the school curriculum to encourage their young girl to reach out into the world in a dynamic way. And of course she had to use reading, speaking, listening, and writing in brain-building ways.

How to Remember More

The academic portion of the American educational experience can be mastered by anyone with a good memory. A's are within the reach of average, motivated girls.

Developing a good memory is quite easy. It's done through learning systems called "mnemonics." It used to be thought that each of our memories was located inside special brain cells called "mneme" cells. The idea is long-since defunct, but the term has lingered to describe a whole range of techniques to improve memory. Many tapes and books are available describing the use of these mnemonic systems, and many are worthwhile. Using a simplified system, any child with average intelligence can, for instance, learn all the presidents of the United States, memorize all the states or provinces, and remember detailed reports and lists. By applying some fun and simple techniques, your daughter's school performance will immediately improve, and you all will have some fun!

A simple mnemonic "peg" system is the most useful device for kids. "Pegs" are groups of objects your daughter already has memorized. By making crazy mental associations and connections to these already remembered items, you are using a peg system of mnemonics.

The lists your girl already has memorized are usually in picture form. Take body parts as an easy example. Most girls can find their toes, knees, stomach, buttocks, hips, and so on. In addition, they can easily visualize these parts in a specific order, for example, top to bottom or large to small. Other lists already packed away in their heads include the faces of family members by age, the houses on their street, the clockwise arrangement of furniture and objects around their rooms, the teachers they've had in their life, and so on. Your daughter can use any of these easy-to-recall lists to help her remember not-so-easy-to-recall information.

The simple peg system you are about to learn works best when using a set of five pegs: five body parts, five pieces of furniture in your daughter's room, five houses on your street—any five things already known. The trick to this mnemonic system is two-fold: First, her pegs must line up in some orderly and reliable way. If you are going to use body parts, start at either the top of the body and work down (head, chest, tummy, knees, toes) or vice versa (toes, knees, tummy, chest, head). If you are going to use furniture as pegs, make sure to go around the room naming them in a set order; either clockwise or counterclockwise works best.

Why such a big deal about an orderly arrangement? The order of pegs must come to mind in an easy and naturally flowing way. Peg systems of memory don't work well if you must constantly struggle to recall the order of the objects that will serve as pegs. If you find that the pegs you've chosen don't flow out naturally and logically ordered for your daughter, shift to a list of pegs that do.

The second trick is to use a wild imagination with this system. The most easily memorized events and facts are those remembered as pictures filled with wild color, sound, weird action, and humor. Memory is no place for conventionality. The weirder the image the more memorable. We are going to ask you to encourage your daughter to let her imagination run wild and really dream up some off-the-wall images.

Here's how you use the system: Let's say for example that your daughter wants to memorize a shopping list (these work great for practice). The list includes toilet paper, peanut butter, bread, milk, and bubble gum. Asking her to just remember these would be difficult for her and surely not fun. Rather, you can have her relate them to a system of pegs. For the purposes of illustration, we'll use the body parts we mentioned in top-down order: head, chest, tummy, knees, and toes.

Combining listed items with the known pegs begins by having your daughter recite the five known body pegs, as we just did, to be certain she remembers them in order. Then take the first item, toilet paper, and ask her to imagine some strange, weird, bizarre, funny, or disgusting way to relate toilet paper with the first peg, her head.

Her machinations might astound you, but the wilder and weirder they are, the easier the facts are to recall later on. Perhaps her invention will be an image of her head wrapped in toilet paper like a mummy. But that's a little too obvious; take it to one higher level of odd and bizarre. Perhaps it will be her head with a toilet paper roll inside with paper rolling out her nose! It could even be weirder, such as flowered toilet paper for hair! The goal here is to have her create something that makes sense to her and make her conjure it up with utter clarity, even if she needs to close her eyes and focus. The more you do this with her, the more natural it becomes. She will easily become creative in useful ways and require less prompting and coaching from you.

The next item on the shopping list is peanut butter. Have your daughter mix the image of her chest (the second peg) with an image of peanut butter. It could be, for instance, that she sees her chest like a fat peanut butter sandwich with the front and rear of her chest as the bread and her middle the peanut butter. Perhaps it might be an even wilder image, in which she takes a huge glob of peanut butter and smears it all over herself and her new clean shirt!—or you doing it to her! Oh my, that would be memorable! Once again, let her make up her own image and visualize it. The wilder it is, the more action it has, and the funnier it is, the easier it will be for her to recall later.

Continue mixing and creating with each of the five items on her list. Then comes the recall part. Have her simply go back and recall the shopping list by looking at the weird pictures she imagined of her head, then chest, tummy, and so on in order. Memory of a list is suddenly and profoundly easy to recall, instantly available, and funny as well! Remember this rule: If she created the pictures, she needn't remember them, because she *knows* them!

We urge you to try this with your daughter today. It rarely fails. Remember that you can remember as much as you have pegs to hang items on. We mentioned earlier the furniture and other noticeable items your daughter has in her room. How many are there? five? ten? Ask her. Assuming your daughter knows five or ten major items scattered around her room, she then has five or ten more pegs to use in addition to the five body pegs we just learned.

How about the arrangement of houses or apartments around your block? How many houses or units are there? ten? fifteen? How are they arranged, starting at your place and going clockwise from your front door? Use the visual memory of those houses, as we did the body parts, to diversify your pool of available pegs. You can simply and quickly develop up to thirty to fifty pegs, but we urge you to start small. We think you'll conclude that inside the head of your daughter are enough memory pegs to take care of any memory need she might have.

You should be aware that other systems of mnemonics exist too. By and large, however, the easiest systems for children to use involve pegs. So learn this simple system and teach it to your daughter, and if time permits, expand your own skill into other areas of memory enhancement. By the way, just to test the power of this system . . . what is the first item on the shopping list?

Active Thinking and Learning

In high school we all learned to read in a thoughtless, semi-hypnotic stupor. We've actually learned to do many of our daily chores on drone mode! Such automatic thinking can be either helpful or damaging depending on how well it's controlled. When it comes to reading and other educational endeavors, we need to teach our daughters to stay in command of their brains. Education only happens for those on their toes and thinking.

We'll be discussing this much more in the creativity chapter, but for now two points deserve mention. First, real learning occurs when learners *engage* the information they're encountering. Real education is not something you get, it's something you do. Whether the "doing" is questioning, finding contradictions, agreeing, finding points of consistency, or immediate application, something must be done on the spot with incoming information or it won't make a difference, much less be learned. The greatest deposit you can make into your daughter's brain trust is that of teaching her to be curious and questioning about the information she encounters. Curiosity and questions are the signs of a live mind.

Second, smartness can be a social disease among girls. Bubble brain. Diz. Airhead. Ditz. Lulu. Dingbat. Doozy. Flake. Ever hear any of these idioms? Do they bring any people to mind? We'll bet over 90 percent of you readers think of girls when reading these words. Why? Because stereotypes don't emerge from vacuums, and too many girls suffer academic anemia as they get older.

To a girl there's a certain stigma about being smart; it's a pressure position. If you'll recall what we learned about a girl's mind as she grows, her desire is to fit in, not stand out. Social pressure creates a problem, especially around the age of puberty, as girls "dumb-down," attempting not to look too smart. Being accepted by peers, and later by boys, is of greater value than being smart.

Research supports this observation. It's well known among educators that around the age of thirteen, girls' scores on standardized tests suddenly drop in math and science. The explanations for this dive typically fault culture-wide sex-bias, but we think the answer is more simple. Eighth grade dumb-down seems to be a highly contagious social disease spread by visual contact. Girls naturally flee the thought of standing out, and when the masses of girls and boys encounter the growing difficulties of higher level math and science, many girls who have the ability to stand out prefer to slip back into the anonymity and acceptance of the masses.

Perhaps the best and easiest way to deal with this problem is by simply putting it on the front burner of conversation and expecting leadership and educational excellence. This scholastic retreat is going to happen to your girl, so prepare yourself ahead of time. Step in and call your daughter up to better academic performance before peer pressure drags her away. You cannot stop peer pressure, but you can influence it far more than you might have heard. If she's left unattended by a parent who's surrendered at the thought of peers' influence, she'll do the easy thing: try to fit in with her peers and not excel. Prevent that by active daily participation in not only her schoolwork, but also her school ambitions.

Building and keeping younger girls sharp and alert is much easier than remediating them once they've grown up. We've noticed that mediocrity has capillary action. For those of you uninitiated, capillary action is the natural attraction a liquid has for a solid that can cause the liquid to move along a hard surface. Some liquids have better capillary action than others, say in the case of WD-40, a well-known lubricant. You can spray this liquid on a solidly rusted nut and bolt, and in just minutes it penetrates through microscopic grooves and holes and actually frees the rusted clump. Just a little dab will travel in many directions.

Allowing the WD-40 of intellectual mediocrity to get established risks capillary movement to other parts of your daughter's life. Make certain you are spending time reading to her, developing her vocabulary and speech skills, and encouraging her to think about themes and morals of stories. Don't allow mediocrity to creep into any cracks. The more natural curiosity and inquisitiveness you show, the more your daughter has the chance of seeing thinking as the normal and fun thing to do. Pressing toward excellence should be expected.

By all means, severely limit your girl's exposure to those elements that destroy her natural curiosity. Unfortunately, chief among the destructors is 99 percent of television and most video games. Video games and T.V. make little girls do exactly the opposite of what they are built to do. While watching, girls sit motionless in one place, stare forward, and don't think. This is not human! Don't allow your daughter to become a couch potato, under any circumstances!

Intervene and provide an environment fertile for thought, experiment, and surprise. Offer her books, art projects, puzzles, field trips (they're not just a school exercise), and plays. Shoot off model rockets, buy a bird and teach it to talk, skip rocks, or take a walk and look for three different kinds of moss. The possibilities are endless! If the kids must watch television, allow us to tell you what we do. We on occasion will tell the kids they can watch one hour of television for every hour of television *they make*. They have to get the video camera out and make a television show or if no camera is available, they can do a one-act play. Guess what happens without fail: They have such a riot creating television that they no longer even think about whatever it was they wanted to see. Now there's a good use of television!

Ordering and Sequencing Your Thinking

Logic is of two varieties, linear and lateral. Linear means "line." Linear logic is the step-by-step thinking that helps us solve problems, determine the most likely reasons for past events, and calculate probable outcomes of what we say and do. Lateral logic is very different and finds its greatest use in the development of creativity and finding new solutions to problems not amenable to linear logic.

Let's focus now on developing linear logic. The links or steps between causes and events are usually obvious to most adults. We all know that we can walk to the nearest door, pull the switch on the wall, and a light will come on. We all learned somewhere in our remote past that some events cause others to happen with near-perfect regularity. Knowing how events will unfold before they happen and understanding how to find order in these events is called logic. Kids teethe on it for years before it assumes the character and functionality adults (most adults) have.

You can begin to teach your daughter to be logical by following a number of suggestions. First, her world must have order for her to learn about order. Order does not come naturally to girls. It is wise to insist on order in how they keep their room (especially toys and clothes), how they prepare for the day (by establishing routines for getting ready for school, etc.), how they plan important activities, and how they attend to their responsibilities. Not to insist on these simple requirements in essence teaches your daughter that order in life is optional. Ask the parents of a girl with no common sense if that's a good thing to teach!

Keep firmly in mind that these guidelines don't actually create common sense or logic in and of themselves. They simply create an atmosphere where logic and order pervade. In the case of girls, immersion in order is a large chunk of learning such order. We're well aware that different girls adapt to order at different speeds. You know your daughter better than anyone, so impose the order at a level just slightly more ordered than her current level. Take it upon yourself to impose some sort of simple routine that has daily repetitions and a predictable nature.

When our kids were small we drew all the items they needed to do in the bathroom in a series of goofy pictures we posted on the bathroom wall. They thought it was fun to follow the routine in the silly way we drew them. There was a series of pictures for the morning and a series for before bed. We've experimented with various mealtime, homework, and television schedules. We've found for us what is the most effective and practical schedule for our team. We encourage you to do the same kind of deliberate experimentation. Predictability is the key. Girls thrive when their world is patterned and predictable.

Second, it's been noted that girls with little common sense get rescued too often. They aren't allowed to sit and simmer and figure problems out for themselves. Remember, where there are no requirements, there is no growth. Let your daughter suffer the indignation and struggle of thinking; it's the best lesson in common sense you could ever offer. If she's stuck, ask her questions that might lead her in a new direction. Don't do the work for her! Encourage her to think, experiment, and gamble on ideas. Start this practice early, and by the time she's old enough to use adult logic, she'll be deft at it.

We play a game in our home called "No Way!" We make some comment, either sensible or completely crazy, and the kids have to decide if we're serious or not. They are encouraged to return volley with a "no way!" if they sense a ruse on our part (which is almost always the case). Consider the following as a simple list you can try immediately:

1. The encyclopedia says the moon is made of cauliflower.
2. Dogs are really overgrown mice.
3. You can use cooked spaghetti noodles for doll hair.

These suggestions are at least thought provoking if not completely wacko! We want the kids to have the freedom to think about what we say and speak up with some backbone if what they're hearing sounds like nonsense. By the way, if they're correct in their objections, we reward them, usually by telling them they can still live with us!

Sometimes we also duel each other in a game we made up called "That's Debatable." What we do is simply find some issue, choose sides, and debate it. We most often play over dinner, and our debates have been known to cover many topics. Nothing is out of bounds, and even if they know nothing of the topic, players are encouraged to make up positions and defend them vigorously. Here's a short list of topics you can try today:

1. Should grade reports be eliminated?
2. Who should be in charge of the house: parents or kids?
3. Who should pick parents' friends?

We try to position the kids to defend a point of view they would not normally take. Rightness and wrongness in these swordfests don't matter to us, only jumping in and playing your hardest with what wits and persuasion you have. It's a riot, and the kids often come up with compelling and fiery arguments. And they've improved through the years.

Thinking is all we're attempting to prompt. We encourage our kids to use logic, but it's more important that they explain themselves with simple ideas that are sensible and consistent. This isn't easy for them. Learning to present ordered and sequenced thoughts with reasoned words is confusing to children. Confusion is a natural predator of reason. Neutralize confusion by encouraging your daughter not to be intimidated by momentary confusion, but to view being stumped and lost as perfectly normal! Girls can easily learn that confusion is the first natural, ordinary step in thinking great thoughts. Teach your girl to think patiently and fearlessly.

Be careful not to make fun of your daughter's thoughtful mistakes. Her machinations are sincere, be they correct or not. All you really want her to do now is participate. She will be highly sensitive about your opinions of her thoughts, so take great care to be supportive and uncritical. Even then she'll probably think you're cross-examining her! Just stay firm and encourage her contributions as much as you can. Keep her talking.

Third, girls must have cause and effect pointed out to them. Children by nature notice events but not the connections between them. Oblivion to the obvious connections between events is common to girls even after many observations and countless explanations. That's why as a therapist I (Bill) frequently heard parents gripe that their girls just had no "common sense." They almost always were referring to the fact that their kids couldn't judge the outcomes of what they were doing, even after repeated coaching.

Among us parents is a belief that our girls should instantly understand what to us is obvious. We tend to get irritated if they don't learn quickly. Learning obvious things is not that easy to a girl. Seeing some rational event pointed out and grasping the cause and effect of what occurred in that event are two different processes. Your daughter will sense your frustration over her not seeing something "so blatant" no matter how well you try to hide it. Your frustration can interfere with her learning. What's required is your surrendering yourself to patience and showing your daughter time after time how cause and effect rules the real world.

One nearly frustration-proof way to point out these logical connections is with pop quizzes. At any particular moment, ask your daughter to explain the outcome of anything she's doing. Use the "if-then" formula: "If you do this, then what will happen?" It's a simple question cutting facets of good thought. Make it a practice, even a habit, to ask for these if-then predictions.

You can ask for if-then predictions in a made-up situation or in real life. A made-up situation might be reading half a story, then having your daughter predict what the ending will be. Ask her to simply think through the story. Try it with weather; can she predict in the morning what the weather will be that evening? Can she predict what she might have for lunch? Mom's disposition? She will make her predictions with glee and may even surprise herself with her own accuracy.

As good as made-up situations are, nothing is quite as good as real life. Once in our local elementary school, I was helping out with a computer class when I saw a little girl pretending to hit the fire alarm. This alarmed me, so I took her aside for some . . . coaching.

"Do you know what happens when you hit that button?"
I asked.

"It makes the bells ring," she said sheepishly.

"Anything else?" I pried.

"Ummmm . . . It makes loud noises."

"Anything else?" I pressed (I was prepared to say this until she'd emptied herself).

"No, I don't think so," she yielded.

With my sternest "Sit down and listen carefully, my dear" voice, I patiently explained that pulling the fire alarm set off a whole chain of bad things, one leading unstoppably to the next. I essentially told her how pulling that lever would lead to the eventual destruction of the universe. In excruciating detail I described how events would deteriorate from pushing a little red button to firemen streaming in from all sides, to kids falling helplessly down stairwells in a frantic melee to escape from the school—a nasty scene all unraveling from a simple, isolated push of a button.

I hope she learned not to press that fire alarm, but let us reiterate that in all likelihood she can't transfer that cause and effect lecture to other areas of her life. For cascading events to form in her brain as a life lesson, she'll need to be shown similar lessons in many different ways. This is where admonitions to think it through come in handy. Ask your daughter to predict what ripples will surge from whatever stones she is about to toss. With some coaching, she can begin to gather the skill of seeing two, sometimes three events beyond any action she takes. That's the ability we call common sense.

The fourth suggestion might be the most critical of all. We learned earlier that the first system of logic children encounter is their language system. Girls who are good in language skills score higher on all measures of cognitive ability than those who aren't. This shouldn't be a surprise. Language is not only powerfully stimulating but also requires the user to follow specific rules. Intensify your efforts to encourage language use, and logic follows as a by-product.

Keep it simple. Not long ago we spoke with a woman whose first daughter had been accepted at Yale University. This was some accomplishment, since this young lady was accepted on academic merit alone with no political connections or favors. The mother was obviously quite proud, so we began to quiz her about this phenomenal achievement.

Our first question was: "What part did you play in her success?" "It's simple," we remember her saying, "I just talked to her every single night." It was stated as if to say, "It was too easy!" We were of course stunned by her intuitive simplicity yet thought there must be something else she'd done. We asked her lots of questions but still got the same answer. Talking every night is all she did. Her intense effort was little more than being interested in and talkative with her girl.

Simply talking to your daughter may not qualify her for an Ivy League education, but the effectiveness of such simple conversation is illustrated in this story. Ask questions, give opinions, or just chat about daily events. If there's magic here, it's in giving your girl a platform upon which to form her own words and thoughts. Pursue simple conversations with your daughter at all ages. Any age is the right age to develop her language skills and thus her logic and common sense.

It might also be instructive to note that our *Girls!* Team has repeatedly remarked on the enormous power fathers had on developing their daughters' common sense and judgment. It may be that men quicken the process of learning logic. Why? There are many possibilities, including their presence and style, their self-confidence in logic, the way they ask questions, or their general way of thinking. What we do know is that there's something special about a man teaching a little girl to think in a systematic way and encouraging her to make good choices. Don't miss the chance to be the man or get a man involved in this part of her growing.

Joie de Vivre

Every child should have an Aunt Marion. My (Kathi's) Aunt Marion had energy, playfulness, and the innocent joy of a child mixed with the wisdom and mature unconditional love of an adult. Her love of life was unrestrained, radiating like rays of warm sunlight into all those around her. She seemed to attack every moment of life. Being with her I found myself filled with sudden bursts of overwhelming anticipation and excitement. I never knew what was going to happen when she was around, but I knew it would be wonderful!

Every bland moment was transformed into something extraordinary when Aunt Marion was there. At the sound of her laughter all the children would rally around her, and the fun would begin. We would form large circles and dance merrily as she initiated silly antics for us to imitate. Our high stepping always ended in gales of laughter. We watched her gymnastic feats with amazement and awkwardly responded to her bubbly challenges to do cartwheels, headstands, and splits. And could she sing! She'd gather us around her piano and belt out one lively song after another. The times never failed to be wild and wonderful. She was beautiful!

Even in the midst of crowding cousins, she made me feel like I was a unique joy to her. She would squeeze my hand, sneak in a hug, or give me a quick wink of the eye that said, "You're special." When I spoke she looked deep into my eyes as though she hung on every word I said. She did hang on every word I said. Her exuberance overflowed into every area of her life. She was *joie de vivre* personified.

Joie de vivre is French for "love of life." Marion and others like her teach us all something special about the look and touch of life. You can have a daughter with all the winning internal qualities of heart and mind, but if she hasn't a spirited joy and happiness, she'll probably end up just another talented robot. "Spirit" hides itself right in front of us, and though we grope about for what we know is right there, we cannot touch it. Yet we know spirit when we see it. Deep in our hearts we hope and pray our daughters have that hot, distinguishing ember of life waiting to flare up within them.

In our church are a number of families with foster children. These kids are generally troubled, and we're patient with them because they've all lived through evil experiences most adults only read about. The men and women bravely stepping in to rescue the lives of these children are saints, and I hope God has something special in store for them. They've earned it.

There is one girl in this gaggle I (Bill) am particularly fond of. She's a seven-year-old with buck teeth and round glasses that continually slide down her nose—a nose, by the way, that's always runny. Her life seems to constantly teeter on the brink of mayhem, but I like her very much. The reason? Whenever she sees me, she attacks me! She hugs me and jumps up and down and gives me things like toys, candy, homemade pictures, and jewelry! She says she's happy to see me and that I make her the happiest girl in the world because I'm there! I'm just a nice man who makes her happy!

Now put yourself in my shoes. Her innocent charms disarm me with regularity (any wonder?). She's a true breath snatcher. The reason is simple and obvious: She is a happy girl and she lets her happiness show in unsophisticated ways. She's the epitome of a spirited girl. She loves life despite all her liabilities. She's one of a kind.

We mention her as another example because this quality of loving life may be difficult to distill conceptually. Once we personify it with the example of a real child, we suddenly see it with clarity. This causes internal leaps and screams of *Yes! That's the spirit I want for* my *girl! I want her happy, energetic, vigorous, audacious, and fearless!* Go ahead, jump up and yell! That's the spirit. Those are good things to want for your girl. It's life!

Most contemporary writers of child development material advocate creating self-reliant children. Self-reliance is a great quality, and we advocate it too. The tendency, however, is to teach parents to base self-reliance on an internal guidance system concocted solely of feelings, intellect, and will. There's nothing wrong with this system; the Achilles heel is that excellence cannot be supported by this triune foundation alone. A broader base is required to cut through life's really tough mustard.

The broader base includes *playfulness, vision,* and *confidence refined into optimism.* These traits can support a bold and daring personality. All three are interdependent. Weaving them into coherence opens girls up to a new sort of life—an adventurous life—going boldly where few people ever go; risking it all in the pursuit of building a masterpiece life; fun-lovingly playing in the big leagues of life, focused on doing exceptional things, fearless in the face of a world sliding down the dark slope of the bell curve. Fun-loving, focused, and fearless: Ahh, now that's joie de vivre!

Fun-loving . . .

Encourage your girl to have fun! This is an important part of the foundation.

The Living Dead

We know a lot of living dead people, but one really stands out in our minds. This fella is a professional with a deadly serious disposition, humorless in every way, and devoid of any interest outside of work. Once we were at an outing at a home adjoining a golf course. It was dusk in the summer, and the sprinkler system had just kicked on all over the course. It was beautiful, and the kids at the gathering all dashed off to watch. We and a few other adults could relate, so we skipped the lingering small talk and raced off with them.

By the time we reached the edge of the property line, a number of the children had already jumped through the sprinklers, inadvertently giving us some fresh ideas. We yelled back to our friend to join us, but he just shook his head and said, "No, I think I'll just pull up a chair here and watch." Sadly, whatever vestige of spirit may at one time have indwelled him had been snuffed out. We, on the other hand, were of the opinion that thirty-five years old is too young to die!

Lighten Up and Have Some Fun!

On occasion we feel prompted to watch the movie *Harold and Maude*. On the surface it's a bit of a morose tale, but the underlying theme is stirring. It's about a rich young man who wants to commit suicide because his life is pointless. He's enamored with death; it seems to him to be the only solution to his sequestered life. He goes to funerals of people he doesn't even know and frequently wanders aimlessly through gray and depressing graveyards.

Then, during one of his cemetery excursions, he meets an old woman named Maude. She's there for a very different reason. She visits there as a reminder that she's still alive. She survived the Nazi death camps and has adopted a view of life as lively as Harold's is macabre.

Their chance meeting was one of vital destiny for Harold. This eighty-year-old woman teaches this very young man how to live life to the fullest. She grows plants, stays up till sunrise, dances to the best of her aging talent, laughs often, and maintains a hysterically funny distaste for convention. She lives! By the end of the movie, you've decided you want to live life like Maude.

Too many girls don't know any live adults. Enjoyment comes by practice, and far too many adults don't practice. The practicing of fun and enjoyment of life can be as responsible for winning in life as all these slick and sensible techniques we've been describing. Just remember that practicing fun starts with your attitude. Lighten up! Find some funny friends, read funny writers, tell a few good jokes! It's great medicine.

Let your daughter have some fun downtime, too. We're sensitive to the charge that some parents just push their kids too much, never letting them have a real childhood. It's been our experience that in nine of ten homes this is not the case; in those homes children aren't pressed nearly hard enough. However, we still suggest that all parents let the kids have some daily fun time with nothing planned at all—serendipity time, if you will, simply letting life unfold in surprising and fun ways.

Let your hair down and just flow with what fun and spontaneous things happen. Let your daughter be a simple child, and you simply be a living adult.

Vapor Trails

I (Bill) once had a man in my life whom I considered a mentor. He had that unique ability to say common things in extraordinarily perceptive ways. He told me once that "even a bad idea, vigorously pursued, can succeed." This statement is innocuous enough until you start to mull it over. At the time, our conversation was revolving around the nature of success and succeeding in the face of stiff opposition. He meant this statement as an encouragement to remain vigilant and energetic no matter how bad the idea or project. He knew that vigor brought the possibility of good things.

This is sage advice not only for whipped entrepreneurs but also for parents of winners. The operative concept here is "vigor" and it is fundamental to developing spirit. Making girls vigorous begins with helping them expend large amounts of energy.

I (Kathi) was once in the audience of a church with a particularly fired-up minister. I must admit I've forgotten much of his lesson, but I can never forget the vivid image he created for how we should leave the building after the service: with fire and smoke billowing off us! It was a colorful and memorable way to describe the kind of excitement we should try to leave in our wake.

We made a decision after that talk that our kids should never leave home in the morning until they had vapor trails streaming off them, just like jets high in the air. Bill created a motivational "Parents' Pledge" and posted it by the front door. We made it a point to take the kids to the door each morning and send them off with some sort of incendiary message of thrill and excitement. It's quickly become a daily habit.

The more energy children expend, the more they have! Have you ever had the experience of physically resting all weekend, but when the week begins you feel tired and restless? That's a strange experience, especially when contrasted with busy weekends doing fun, vigorous activity that leaves you feeling . . . refreshed and enlivened! The only way to explain it is to conclude that lively, expensive (meaning spending lots of energy) living creates energy. We need to teach this conclusion to our children and encourage them to spend their lives in wild quantities!

If you are really interested in gaining energy, you must vigorously spend what you have. We emphasize this point because so many sedentary, effortless options for our time exist. It's not natural to conserve youthful energy, and those interested in developing girls bursting with spirit and life should pump up the voltage. Make high-wattage recreation such as running, climbing, jumping, hopping, skipping, screaming, tumbling, laughing, and boxing a requirement.

Girls who recreate have different outlooks and attitudes than those allowed to store their energy like D-cells in skirts. Think of ruddy-faced, dirty, sweaty, smiling soccer players versus vacant-eyed, expressionless T.V. addicts. Who has the real life? Who has the valence? Who's spending it and who's storing it? What's best is that getting girls to expend energy doesn't require thumbscrews; girls will do it without pressure if just given the chance. Create the energy-spending options and step back! Watch the beauty of youthful energy.

Focused . . .

Is there anything that really excites you about living? If not, find something. Everybody has big problems, and few people really care about yours. Those are the facts, and to expect anything more is foolish. Don't excuse yourself from stepping boldly forward and living in spite of pain. That's what adulthood is about. Stop talking to yourself, accept the confusion and pain, and seize your life!

Is this too harsh? Have you ever heard of Barbara Johnson? There are few people holding this book whose pain can compare to hers. Yet she's written some of the most popular and touching motivational books we've ever read.

Consider these facts. Her husband was involved in a car wreck that left him near death at first and vegetative for months. Her oldest son was killed in Vietnam. Her next son was killed in a head-on crash by a drunk driver. Her next son announced his homosexuality and hid incommunicado for years in the gay community. Had enough? There's one more thing: She's been diagnosed as having adult-onset diabetes, which is not as severe as the juvenile form but is nevertheless life-threatening.

Has she cried? Countless times. She's felt depressed, tired, and abandoned and then gone on to write upbeat books with promising titles like *Momma Get the Hammer, Fresh Elastic for Stretched Out Moms, Splashes of Joy in the Cesspools of Life,* and *Stick a Geranium in Your Hat and Be Happy!*

How can you start living this victoriously today? Take time to find something to be joyful about each day. It might be a beautiful rosebud, a bird singing outside your window, a call from a friend. Focus on and celebrate these highlights. Teach your daughter to do the same.

You Are Your Daughter's Window

You face choices about what you will show your girl. We strongly urge you to show her good, exciting things no matter how hard it may be to find positives. What is real to your girl is what she hears coming out of your mouth and what actions of yours she witnesses.

She can only be as unflagging as you show her to be. Your vision of what she can be represents the upper limit of her childhood potential. The power you have in this regard reminds us of the poignant and bittersweet story of *The Window* by G. W. Target:

> There were once two men, both seriously ill, in the same small room of a great hospital. Quite a small room, just large enough for the pair of them—two beds, two bedside lockers, a door opening on the hall, and one window looking out on the world.
>
> One of the men, as part of his treatment, was allowed to sit up in bed for an hour in the afternoon (something to do with draining fluid from his lungs), and his bed was next to the window.
>
> But the other man had to spend all his time flat on his back—and both of them had to keep quiet and still. Which was the reason they were in the small room by themselves, and they were grateful for the peace and privacy—none of the bustle and clatter and prying eyes of the general ward for them.
>
> Of course, one of the disadvantages of their condition was that they weren't allowed to do much: no reading, no radio,

certainly no television—they just had to keep quiet and still, just the two of them.

Well, they used to talk for hours and hours—about their wives, their children, their homes, their jobs, their hobbies, their childhood, what they did during the War, where they'd been on vacations—all that sort of thing. Every afternoon, when the man in the bed next to the window was propped up for his hour, he would pass the time by describing what he could see outside. And the other man began to live for those hours.

The window apparently overlooked a park, with a lake, where there were ducks and swans, children throwing them bread and sailing model boats, and young lovers walking hand in hand beneath the trees, and there were flowers and stretches of grass, games of softball, people taking their ease in the sunshine, and right at the back, behind the fringe of trees, a fine view of the city skyline.

The man on his back would listen to all of this, enjoying every minute—how a child nearly fell into the lake, how beautiful the girls were in their summer dresses, then an exciting ball game, or a boy playing with his puppy. It got to the place where he could almost see what was happening outside.

Then one fine afternoon, when there was some sort of parade, the thought struck him: Why should the man next to the window have all the pleasure of seeing what was going on? Why shouldn't he get the chance?

He felt ashamed, and tried not to think like that, but the more he tried, the worse he wanted a change. He'd do anything.

In a few days, he had turned sour. He should be by the window. And he brooded, and he couldn't sleep and grew even more seriously ill—which none of the doctors understood.

One night as he stared at the ceiling, the other man suddenly woke up coughing and choking, the fluid congesting in his lungs, his hand groping for the button that would bring the night nurse running. But the man watched without moving.

The coughing racked the darkness—on and on—choked off—then stopped—the sound of breathing stopped—and the man continued to stare at the ceiling.

In the morning, the day nurse came in with water for their baths and found the other man dead. They took away his body, quietly, no fuss.

As soon as it seemed decent, the man asked if he could be moved to the bed next to the window. And they moved him, tucked him in, and made him quite comfortable, and left him alone to be quiet and still.

The minute they'd gone, he propped himself up on one elbow, painfully, laboriously, and looked out the window.

It faced a blank wall.

This story illustrates a simple principle. Your girl sees a great deal of life through your eyes. What you see and what you tell her you see matter deeply. Make certain she experiences some happiness, excitement, anticipation, joy, and love. With your help she will begin to see them clearly.

. . . and Fearless

In many respects this book is about building self-confident girls. Do you remember the childhood game of saying a word over and over until it ceased to have any meaning? The truth of the game doesn't stop at kindergarten. If we say or hear one word too often, it stops having meaning to our minds. Such is the problem we face with the powerful but diluted word *confidence*.

When we refer to building fearless girls, the word *confidence* (however diluted and overused) pops to mind. We would urge you to consider changing this knee-jerk associa-. tion slightly: Replace the word *confidence* with *optimism*. *Indefatigable optimism* might even be better. This is an optimism that believes that no risk is too great, that ignores the finger waggers and naysayers, that is rooted not solely in self-reliance (though that's important) but in relentless faith. This faith must be in something bigger than oneself, something immeasurably good and unstoppable. Such faith lies at the center of any confident girl.

Creating a focused optimism can happen many ways. We think that a natural way is to expose your daughter to two different types of women and restrict her exposure to a third. The first kind of woman is one who is exceptionally old but still full of spit and sass. The second kind is a woman who has fought battles and is either at the top or on the fast track to doing something exceptional. Limit your daughter's exposure to the third kind: the handwringer.

Like Aunt Marion, older women with some "juice" left are a heart lift. Their lives vibrate with a magic every girl needs to touch. We are hard pressed to explain it but we know the net effect of this sort of exposure is significant. You are going to have to search for women like this, but they're around.

These women are always eager to take part in the life of a child. It's part of their interpersonal magnetism. As a child, I (Bill) remember my mom spending time with an elderly woman named Germaine. It makes me smile just saying her name! She was a cashier at the local drug store and she was a hoot. I can still see her clever eyes dancing as she offered us gum and laughter and priceless advice about everything. We would go to her house, and she'd make us chili; she'd show us her rifles and play her busted up piano. She'd sing with a screechy voice that only kids could love, and when she was done she'd spin tall tales and goad us to stand up to bullies. We loved that woman. My life is richer for what little time we had with her before she died. Every little girl needs a Germaine. Recruit one.

In similar fashion, try to arrange a meeting between your daughter and a woman who is moving and making things happen with her life. She will form a reference point for your girl. Such women have an air about them that your daughter ought to feel. She'll remember it for a long time.

There are plenty of these women around. The problem will be getting their attention or time. We've found that if you tell them what you are doing and what you are trying to accomplish, they will be gracious and extend themselves to you and your daughter. Perhaps you would like to help your daughter prepare some questions to ask this woman, such as: What makes you so excited?, What's the craziest thing you ever did?, Do you have any advice for a future "wonder woman" like me? and so on. Simply plant the idea into your daughter that she can ask questions.

Now, for the Henny Pennys. You remember Henny Penny; she was the fabled chicken who always thought the sky was falling. The poor thing! What torture! Take it on yourself to counteract those who fear failure and run around constantly wringing their hands in fear of what might happen. Help find friends and mentors for your daughter who are not slowed down by fears. Encourage her to be risky and audacious. Grant her constant support in trying the impossible and ignoring those who would dash the hope and spirit you've labored so hard to create.

Your girl is an investment to protect. Just keep in mind that most of those with whom she interacts on a daily basis are filled with fear and pessimism. Pessimism, like mediocrity, can step into a girl's life and handicap her potential. Encourage your daughter to charge into life with youthful vision and passion.

We're reminded of the touching story of 1994 Miss America Heather Whitestone. Deaf since the age of one-and-a-half, Ms. Whitestone has climbed a mountain few ever even attempt. She needed six years of speech therapy just to learn to say her last name! Her secret? "The most handicapped people in the world are negative thinkers," she says. As a child, her mother told her the last four letters of "American" are "I can."

"There are no limitations now," says her mother, Debbie Braidi. "When the going gets tough, you just look at Miss America and say, '*She* can do it.'"

Part **3**

Building
Extraordinary
Behaviors

Life Control through Self-Control

I (Bill) will never forget the day I realized the need to teach my daughter self-control. She was about three or four, and we were at the park playing. I had returned to the car with her in tow and rounded the rear of the car with intentions of opening up the trunk. I never made it that far. She followed me around the rear of the car and suddenly broke into a hand-on-hip, saucy little swagger that makes fathers' hair stand on end!

"Well, Hi," she breathed.

Ahh!!! I must have looked like Barney Fife, ogling in disbelief. What was I seeing? Where did she see *this*?! Cute is cute, but hot is out! It was a freakish, twilight-zone moment for me. *Now what do I do?* I wondered.

Thankfully, she answered the question by scrunching her shoulders in feigned shame, then bursting out in laughter and running around the car to retrieve her dolls. The moment was all quite innocent but left lingering questions that I as a young father had never asked. Is this some kind of female thing? Does she know what she's doing? Should I worry? It's funny; I didn't remember seeing three-year-olds act that way when I was young. Why, in my neighborhood we were more interested in keeping our diapers on. Yet I knew times were changing. I felt the sudden need to buy a shotgun.

I pacified myself thinking that we could teach her to control herself in the future. I hoped *far* into the future! Well, as we've since learned, growing girls don't allow for much procrastination. The first hints of any new development usually indicate more are not far behind. Thankfully, Jessie's coquettish slink hasn't returned, but the need to teach her self-control has.

A Simple Premise

We want to base this chapter on a simple premise: *It is our daughter's responsibility eventually to do something with her own life.* She needs to seize it! Think about your own successes for a moment. Did anything good ever happen because your mom or dad paved the road for you with rose petals? No! Your successes happened because you seized control of yourself and your situation, worked hard with a vision in mind, and made it happen.

It makes sense to us that nothing of real value or purpose happens in your girl's life unless she learns to manage her own life. Life management begins with girls learning simple self-control. They must learn to control their bodies, actions, expressions of emotion, and so on. As they grow, this self-control must be applied to uncomfortable circumstances they would rather avoid. Enduring difficulty with self-control and focus is called self-discipline.

Self-control is taught in an escalating series of skills beginning with rudimentary body control (not wetting herself, eating with a fork) and progressing to high-level self-discipline (studying trigonometry, being patient in a relationship that is challenging). These skills are learned by doing, and you must be your daughter's catalyst.

Making our girls control themselves and develop discipline is not popular. Not long ago we heard a professional football player remark that he wants his newborn daughter to grow up "totally uninhibited." The more you think about this statement the more stunning it seems. We all want our girls to experience the joy of freedom. That's normal and good. But reams of psychological data suggest that children who are happiest are those who live with consistent rules and expectations. It appears that raising a totally uninhibited girl would depress the chances for her happiness and success! Do your part and make her learn some things.

The Telescopic View

What we are really trying to do here is build girls who can some time in the future *make themselves do difficult things.* There are many activities that are uncomfortable or painful or take time and effort, but are done because of the benefit derived. That's called self-discipline. Self-discipline requires long-term development, blending three major ingredients:

1. Maturity
2. Significant emotional stability
3. Self-control

Since we're talking here about little girls, we think it safe to say the first two, maturity and emotional stability, are still way off over the horizon, even though we see glimpses of them from time to time. Our best efforts should be directed to teaching the last quality, self-control.

Over what should girls exercise self-control? This list would be a great start:

Anger and temper
Attitudes
Chores

Eating habits
Leadership with peers
Movements and physical reactions
Personal hygiene
Sharing with others
Tidiness with possessions and in their room
Truthfulness
Sibling conflicts
Table manners
Poise in social situations
Self-confidence

This is a wide assortment of aspects of life in which your girl should exercise self-control, but there could be many more. Because of the size of the potential list, we've decided, rather than delve into each of these topics, to discuss four basic principles that over time build self-control. In combination they create self-control in all the areas listed above. Teach these well and your daughter will continue on toward strong self-discipline.

Be Disciplined Yourself

Though at times it's difficult, we've tried to avoid talking about parents. This book is about girls, so conversations about us adults don't always mesh in well. However, this is one area where we need to focus specifically on you and what role you play in teaching self-control.

By far, your greatest gift to a girl's development of self-control is your own self-discipline. It's obvious to most that having ourselves under consistent control is vital. But we compromise ourselves too often. We get caught up in the hurricane of life, becoming pieces of debris blown hither and yon by forces we are unprepared to handle. And little eyes are watching it all. Our girls are learning simple lessons we may wish they hadn't seen. We may be accidentally planting little weed seeds.

Work on making yourself consistent and steady. You don't have to be perfect in this, but be vigilant to be on time for events, do what you say you'll do, make your yes be yes and your no be no. Be visibly organized with your daily life, keep your things where they belong, maintain good hygiene, dress up from time to time, be a standard of wisdom, prudence, and good taste. Keep yourself above senseless arguments, use your maturity and vision, plan ahead, and know as much as possible where you are going. Follow these rules and you position yourself to be the beacon directing your daughter past her storms onto the calmer waters of self-control.

Remember, your daughter is only dimly aware of herself and lives in a world that to her has no tangible future or past. Her life is now. She is impulsive by nature and subject to acting without thought of the next moment. It's difficult to conceive of her having a great deal of self-control or self-discipline under these dynamic, reactive conditions! As a matter of fact, your girl won't learn much self-control without you. What she is able to learn later on will only come by great effort. You would do both of you a great favor by helping her build self-control in small and concrete ways.

Some time during the first five or so years of life, your being in control of her life changes to her controlling her own life. Both of you want that transition to take place. Control shifts gradually. With you trying to relinquish control slowly and her trying to seize it away quickly, this transition of power creates frequent jolting and lots of friction.

Parental expectations and goals change over the course of this transition. Subtly, parents drift from wanting little missy to stop putting chocolaty fingers on the wallpaper to insisting she control her tongue, do her chores, watch her attitude, maintain composure and poise in a crisis, and so on. As your expectations of her become vastly more complex, your parenting style needs to mature as well. Maintain your own self-confidence and your focus as your daughter gradually learns to control her life.

Teach Her to Contain Herself

By now you may have noticed that we don't talk much about corrective discipline in this book. That is because by and large parents are more interested in motivating their girls than controlling their bad behavior. It's as if control is not a big challenge compared to spurring them on. So, we'll not spend much time on this topic except to describe how self-containment can help a girl focus her energies specifically.

Youthful energy is like a big ball of sunlight. Rays emanate from this ball like bright spokes. Our image of self-control is taking all the radiating light and corralling it into a narrow path pointing in some specific direction—to *contain* the energy and focus it.

Teaching girls to contain their own hot source of energy is part of the big picture of creating long-term self-control. Containment precedes any form of education. Containment precedes socialization. Containment precedes any kind of learning at all. That's why helping girls contain and focus their energy is vital for their building a base of knowledge and experience.

How do we teach containment? It all begins with acclimating girls to barricades. Nobody ever seized life who didn't first learn to obey some strict rules of conduct. Barricades take the form of a few simple rules of conduct. It seems to make little difference what exactly the rules are that you impose. Don't try to create an overbearing, stifling set of rules, but a matter-of-fact and natural set of boundaries. Rules are normal, but rules for rules' sake are silly. Do your best to have them make some sense, and do what you can to explain their purpose. You don't want her to slam into the rules, only be guided by them. Rules such as "No talking back," "No television after 8:00 P.M. on school nights," "No missing homework assignments," and the like work well. Make this a set of no-budge, no-apology rules that fairly reflect what you expect of your daughter. Then *point your girl down a path to self-control.*

We stress obedience to the rules rather than threats of punishment. We should say that we have no problem with the idea of punishment. If you think about it, "consequences" are just a sugared up, politically correct way of saying "punishment." So let's not get bogged down in the words. Our approach assumes that the kids wouldn't even dream of breaking a rule. By our attitude we communicate that rules are for the common good, and it's an exciting opportunity to be able to live under them! It works.

Take care to list, clarify, and give concrete examples of the consequences of or punishments for breaking the rules: "Talking back will require an apology" or "Unapproved television will mean a twenty-four-hour T.V. holiday" or "Missing homework assignments will require an extra half-hour of study per night." Again, make these specific, concrete, and foreknown.

Insisting on firm barricades brings us to that first immutable law of teaching self-control: Girls don't like being controlled. As girls become more competent at running small portions of their own lives, they think they deserve all the control immediately. The friction caused by encounters with your controls can take the form of screaming, fits of red-faced, frothy-mouthed anger, accusations, complaining, and general unhappiness. There's no avoiding this occasional reaction stemming from efforts to control young girls. These tell-tales of friction usually mean something good is happening.

All personal transformation at any age is accompanied by discomfort and stretching. The common reaction for any of us made to stretch is to resist, usually in some form of anger. This is especially so with little girls. If you remain firm in your convictions, good things will happen. Take her resistance as a litmus test of her normality. Our goal is both to teach her about control and to control her at the same time. To that end, expend some effort to make the legal system comprehensible to her, *and* expect some friction too.

One of our *Girls!* Team members tells a funny friction story. It seems that one day she scolded her eight-year-old daughter for some violation of house rules. As eight-year-olds do, her daughter packed up a small suitcase of clothes, a little lunch, and ran away from home. She got as far as the front tree, which she climbed up and perched in. She sat there in the crotch of some limbs for a long time—long enough, as it turns out, that her mother was able to sneak up and get a picture! That picture has become a family heirloom and treasure, bringing the family repeated pleasure and laughter.

Teach Her Internal Locus of Control

A number of years ago, psychologists were searching for better explanations for why people get depressed. They picked an interesting place to search: where people place the blame for things that go wrong for them. What the scientists found was provocative, for they discovered that people who are most often depressed tend to feel out of control and that life just "happens." Life for them is a mysterious steward of surprises, most of which are bad and unwanted. Control in their lives resides externally, outside of themselves someplace.

Happy people have a very different view. To them, action in life is centered in themselves and the efforts they put forth. Control is internal. The locus of control is within, and *they* make decisions and create the action that shapes their destiny. There are simply few situations in which these men and women don't feel they could have a personal impact on what is happening. What you believe about who or what controls your life determines how you will feel about yourself and determines your chances for happiness and satisfaction.

What we've only recently begun to appreciate is that many girls grow up believing that the good and bad things in life come primarily from external sources, like schools, parents, and friends or peers, over which they have no control. They learn, in essence, that they can do little to shape their own lives. Is it any wonder that some give up and don't do the things necessary to seize initiative in life? The best reason to write this chapter is to help girls discover that the source (locus) of decision making is in them.

Where do we begin the process of teaching our girls internal locus of control? One of the great early lessons from the research was that some people learned early in life to blame sources outside themselves for their own failures and mistakes. Excuse-making had grown from childhood onward. The blaming was active and aggressively negative.

These people can never be convinced they are at fault for anything, because they believe the cause of problems is everyone and everything else! They believe others are causing all the ripples in life that roll over them like gigantic, unstoppable waves. This thinking is virulent and must be stopped or your girl will become a chronic excuse-maker seeking to skirt responsibility for everything. Successful people take responsibility for the good and bad things that happen to them.

Help your daughter assume responsibility for her mistakes quickly. The longer she dwells on mistakes and poor judgments the more perspective she loses. Make certain she understands that mistakes aren't bad. They are a normal part of life. People shrug off responsibility for their own actions most often because of a belief that weakness or mistakes are unfixable and infinitely damaging. The thought of something so awful or embarrassing is unacceptable to them, so they constantly dodge responsibility. Making mistakes isn't so awful, and now is the time to teach that it isn't. Mistakes are just mistakes, weaknesses just weaknesses, and rather than ignore or deny them, your girl is wisest to acknowledge them quickly and use them as an energy source to propel new decisions and personal change.

We are fond of asking kids who come to us admitting a mistake or moaning about an intractable problem, "So, what are you going to do about it?" We don't yell or pound our fists or twitch with fury. Our question suggests to them that their problem is fixable and they had better begin thinking. A problem is just something to fix.

There's another source of power in admitting mistakes quickly and completely: Girls who are unafraid of the embarrassment of mistakes take more risks. Quick admissions of blame eliminate extensive embarrassment and will more quickly get your daughter to fearlessly surge forward. Can you see how girls reared embarrassment-free don't necessarily have to know how to do something ahead of time in order to try it? There's much less to fear. Since they see nothing for themselves to lose, they become experimenters and attempters. Teach your girl to live life on the offensive, come what may.

There is one technique I evolved in my practice that's remarkably effective in building internal locus of control, particularly with younger girls. I call it the "One Discrete Problem/One Discrete Solution" approach (ODP/ODS). It's rooted in some simple observations that when potential self-control situations are broken down into itsy-bitsy, teeny-weeny (that's girl lingo for *discrete*) pieces, all girls will grab control of themselves and extend their control further.

Girls face problems controlling themselves in many situations because the action of those moments pass by too quickly. They get confused and overwhelmed. When the self-control problem is redefined into a teeny-weeny item, the solution clearly defined, and the time needed to apply the fix just a few seconds at a specific moment, girls can control themselves very well. They can learn terrific life control by first learning this form of event control.

Your daughter can be coached to find one very clear, simple problem of self-control to fix. Let's take one off the earlier list. Let's say she needs more self-control in personal tidiness. This is a rather enormous problem to tackle, especially if she's in the habit of being a pig. Any comments with a pig reference will baffle and irritate her, not clarify or motivate her! Rather than being overwhelmed with the enormity of "Clean up your life, Oinky!" she can methodically break the problem down and focus herself on fixing just one small part, say for example how her bed is made.

By focusing her down to one discrete problem in self-control, a messy bed, and one discrete solution, making her bed each morning, she can generate a specific, clearly defined, and tailor-made action rather than slipping into her otherwise pigsty-like ways. This success in focusing greatly boosts her sense of internal locus of control. Placing this whole ODP/ODS fix in the context of time—say, encouraging her to make her bed in no more than fifteen seconds—allows her to know the feeling of full internal control through a carefully orchestrated experience set in time.

Do this exercise often and she'll quickly carry over self-control to areas that previously stymied and frustrated her. We recently were consultants in a situation that nicely illustrates this ODP/ODS approach. A quiet young girl, age ten, in a family we know was having problems interacting in public with adults other than her parents. She would become silent and intimidated in the presence of an adult and stay close to her parents without saying a thing. It was actually rude, and the parents wanted some ideas about what to do.

We suggested that the little girl focus all her efforts on one discrete part of the problem: introducing herself. Rather than trying to make this kid Miss Manners in one whack, we suggested that she focus all her efforts on shaking hands. No talking, no eye contact, no witty repartee—just shake. This solution defined the problem in simple terms and identified the fix in a very easy maneuver taking less than five seconds. We got her to agree that she could do that and had her practice several times for us. She was superb.

We suggested that the parents run through the fix with her several times, then go find a situation to test it out. The parents did so, and to their amazement their daughter did what she had never before done: She shook! Certainly to us this is no big deal, but to this girl and her parents it was monumental! It was certainly not magic. It was as simple as focusing her attention on one simple dimension, then making her responsible for it alone. It was self-control pure and simple, and her excitement from managing this previously confusing and intimidating problem was a treat to see!

Self-Control Is Self-Rewarding

Thankfully, most self-control is self-rewarding. Girls able to handle themselves get invited to spend the night more frequently by friends, receive more privileges at school, have a wider peer group, and are invited to do more with family members. To the best of your ability try to help your daughter enjoy the fruit of her own self-control by helping her get places, showing interest in her activities, and letting her know you are proud of her.

Believe it or not, most girls respond well to a simple pat on the back. What happens is that in our busy lives we fail to take note of the self-controlling, self-disciplining things our girls do on their own. Take some time to make special note of those situations you can find in which your girl went above and beyond or simply handled herself properly, even if it was something quite insignificant. Her acts of self-control are no small matter to her, and you should at least recognize them with a smile and congratulations!

There are other more creative ways to reward your daughter's self-control. Take her places with you and show her off! Buy her small tokens and gifts to express your appreciation! Let her know specifically what she did that made you so proud. Participate with her in her favorite activities (this is highly rewarding). Allow her to or suggest she participate in events or activities that would clearly be off-limits to those of lesser control. Be imaginative. Go out of your way to create an award.

A Four-Part Harmony

Integrating these elements involved in self-control takes time. You may have many of these elements in place already. Use this chapter to focus your efforts and sharpen up some of the interventions that already exist in your home. Prepare yourself for some discomfort and second-guessing along the way. Nobody has ever helped a girl meet the challenge of excellence who didn't at some point wonder if he or she were doing the right thing. You are.

Girltalk

Married Four Times before Lunch

I (Bill) recently had a strange experience when going to our kids' elementary school on a quick errand. I found the boys doing their things (combat games such as prison battleball and football, complete with first-grade trash talk and taunting) and girls doing their things (jump rope and monkey bars).

One group of girls caught my attention because they were standing in a close huddle, arm in arm, whispering and gesturing with great animation. It was a private little group that had something very intense going on. Breaking the huddle, they dashed to the foot of the school steps, holding hands, looking at each other, and screaming madly. One girl in this sixsome climbed high up the concrete steps, turned her back majestically to the crowd, and threw her coat over her shoulder to the others. They scrambled and screamed as one girl grabbed the coat and ran. The other girls quickly encircled her and rehuddled, congratulating her, whispering, jumping up and down, and playing with her hair!

Huh? Being a guy, I thought playgrounds were places to demonstrate manhood, not to gather together, talking and giggling.

I was able to catch one of these little squealies long enough to ask her what the game was. "We're throwing wedding bouquets to each other," she said. "Whoever catches the bouquet is going to get married, and all the other girls want to talk and dance with her! I've been married four times so far and *it's not even lunch yet!*"

Girltalk! Most girls talk a lot! They talk in the mornings; they talk in the afternoons and evenings. They talk about their own lives, they gossip, they flit from and light on topics here and there, laugh about some troubles, and sob in each other's arms about other troubles. Your girl's a conversation machine. Don't be fooled by her occasional silences, her strategic coyness, or long bouts of introspection. She loves to talk; it's a girl's gateway to the world of relationships. By the time she reaches adulthood, she will have long since figured out how to create action using words. She'll be surgical in her capacity to verbally relate, drawing people in or shutting them out as she chooses.

Since talking is central to your daughter's young life, your mastering the talk game is a premier opportunity for building a dynamic relationship with her. We want you to be successful with that opportunity. Let's reiterate our mission statement for this book: *to successfully describe what girlhood is like and to define what parents must do to help their girl become an extraordinary woman.* In regard to communication, you must improve your abilities and teach her to improve hers.

A Quick Primer

Girls use words to get connected to others. Words are bridges. Girls speak as a way of soothing dreaded loneliness. Words are much more than commands and requests; they are elemental connections without which a girl's spirit dies. Giving and taking words are like passing precious gifts to others.

Most mothers know all this and respond aptly. Fathers, on the other hand, roam another range. To men, words are steely cold, just tools to be used and ignored with equal indifference. Little of a man's soul traverses to another person through words. Men use words not to commune but to command, inquire, and request.

Such a methodical chill is alien to girls. Coldness is what they seek to escape, and with all their savvy they try to warm up interpersonal voids with words gleaming with fusion. This warm-up goes on nonverbally, too, with snuggling, gift giving, touching, and paying attention. All these activities are unstoppable natural female tendencies. Grasp the focus of this attentiveness and you find a hint of what girls are trying to accomplish. Girls naturally gravitate toward anyone who links with them on these verbal and nonverbal levels.

The two-way linkage is normal and natural, but not simple! Heed this warning: Girltalk has strict rules and cycles that advance in complexity from birth through adulthood. The trick is to get into this cycle while the opportunity for interaction is at its peak. Your daughter will develop her own style early and shape it and hone it over the years. Getting to know her style paves the way for effective interaction with her. But it is you who must understand and adapt to what's going on and adjust to what's evolving. You can do that.

Communication Skills

Take note that because of girls' love of relationships, communicating effectively is one of the easier things you are going to work on together. She'll take to it like a bird to flight. The following is a potpourri of communication skills to teach your girl and use yourself to better communicate with her. Teach them, use them, and then stand back and watch her soar.

- Speak with an animated voice
- Give gifts and exchange compliments
- Use touch to communicate

- Use appropriate formalities
- Express anger effectively
- Express opinions clearly
- Express self-satisfaction appropriately
- Ask for what you want
- Stand up for yourself
- Ask productive questions
- Talk with her

Speak with an Animated Voice

We can think of dozens of situations in which an animated voice is helpful. Animation in this sense is the quality of liveliness and variability in the sound of one's voice. Your daughter can easily learn to control the speed, tone, pitch, volume, and projection of her voice. And she'll love to practice!

There are many benefits to helping your daughter create this ability. First, controlling her voice allows her to have greater impact when she talks. It also makes it more likely that she will be able to attract and hold listeners, and in subtle ways animation makes her message more powerful. But that's not all.

An animated voice may be most helpful for girls who are frustrated by their inability to express themselves. The ability to express themselves and feel understood is vital to girls. Much of this expressiveness is not in the words they use but in the way they speak—the tones, inflections, speed, loudness, pronunciation, dialect. Expressiveness is all learned.

A great way to teach your girl to speak with animation is by encouraging make-believe conversations or practicing anticipated ones. We have a rule in our house that nobody is allowed to ask for anything in a mealy-mouthed way—you know, the sorry-old-me whine that sounds more like bleating. When we first noticed our kids doing this singsong routine we held a practice session to get them accustomed to speaking with dignity and confidence. "Come before us boldly," we instructed. We told them to lower the tone of their voices, stick out their chins, and project their voice with slow, measured assurance. It was cute and worked well!

Girls love this sort of instruction. Tell your girl that her voice is like an instrument and on that instrument she can play a wide variety of tunes she never thought she could play. Tell her for instance to speak quietly, then scream suddenly; to use a high-pitched voice, then a deep and resonant one; to speak quickly, then slowly; to speak at first in an even and monotone fashion, then stutter. As she alters and animates her voice in several ways, her communication will be infinitely better and more interesting.

Give Gifts and Exchange Compliments

Little girls love to give things. Giving is part of their nature. When a small girl brings you a flower, it comes from a deep part of her soul. Gifts from girls are extensions of their love and admiration. Words are gifts, too. When you speak to your girl, she considers it a special gift. When words come from her, well, that's a gilded gift! Compliments are powerful expressions that launch from and land deep in her heart.

For weeks, whenever I (Kathi) picked up our son Zac at his friend's house, the boy's little sister would always smile at me. She was a smallish four- or five-year-old with long blond hair and a sheepish nature. Though I'd try to chat with her, she'd scurry behind her mom's legs and peer elfenlike from behind the safety of maternal kneecaps.

One day as I entered the house, she dashed by me and picked up a small chalk drawing she'd made. She came back, handed it to me, then hastily retreated to Mommy's knees. I raved for several moments about her artistic talent, then put the picture down and left. Little did I know at the time what a faux pas I'd committed.

On my next visit, the whole scenario was repeated with a bit of a twist. Her mother informed me that after I'd left the last time, my little friend had cried and cried because I'd not taken her drawing! On hearing this news, I bent down and promised her I wouldn't forget, thanking her profusely for her lovely gift. To my shock, she dashed from around her mother's legs and gave me a big hug! Then she ran off and retrieved a postage-stamp-sized school picture of herself and gifted me with it as well.

Encourage your daughter to actively participate in all sorts of gift giving, and do it yourself too. Notice her small, seemingly insignificant efforts to give you something, and don't allow a gift to be passed without singling out the giver as special. Make flattering remarks to your girl frequently, and show her opportunities to do the same to others. If by chance the receiver of her gift or compliment fails to adequately thank her, you pour it on! What matters is for girls to overcome natural shyness and learn to be comfortable with giving themselves through special gifts and by making positive and gracious statements to others.

Use Touch to Communicate

We know how this sounds like Currier and Ives, but a child snuggled in its parent's arms is a warm sight. There's some sort of magic in the human touch. Whether it's kissing ouchies, caressing ruffled hair, squeezing plump little arms, or even rubbing a tiny little back, touch talks.

Touch impacts conversations too. Touch is a multiplier for talking. That's a fancy way of saying that whatever you speak with your lips is made more pronounced and memorable when you add some sort of physical contact. We think parents must learn to be more deliberate in their physical contact with their daughters. Hug them often, whisper secrets in their ears, rub their shoulders, and in all ways impose your presence on them physically as you speak.

Our kids are so used to this that they warn us when they don't want to be touched. I (Bill) am a runner, and sweat pours off me like a waterfall whenever I jog. The sweatier the better as far as I'm concerned, because when I get done I hug everybody who ventures close to me. Yes, it's gross, and they love it! One particular morning Jessie met me on the stairs and seeing me began to back away quickly. "Look, Dad," she said. "You just stay away from me. . . . I'm having a great day so far, and my hair is perfect!" In violation of my own solemn vow to touch the lives of my children, I kept the gooey sweat to myself.

Become known as the parent who isn't afraid to physically touch his or her kids. Be known as the family that holds hands, walks arm in arm, tickles, and pats. In the process you'll set a standard other families will admire and copy.

Not long ago we had family closeness modeled for us. We were shopping in the local supermarket when appearing before us was a clump of people all walking arm in arm. It looked like a rugby scrum, for they were swaying back and forth between the bleach and the brillo pads, laughing and giggling. They were enjoying time together without the slightest hint of self-consciousness. It was, of all people, our family pediatrician and her three adult children. Suddenly, all her excellent advice and superb professional training meant less to us than the life she was modeling before us there in the soap aisle. Her actions spoke convincingly. Whatever she was doing with her kids, we wanted to do it too. At that moment she could have told us that drinking toilet bowl cleaner would create family closeness and we would've grabbed a jug!

Don't underestimate your power to show others the right way to interact with your daughter. Hug her, touch her, and send a message of health to a world starved for some contact.

Use Appropriate Formalities

Formal graces are the simple verbal condiments of social interaction. Few things charm us like a polite and socially adept young girl. We are referring here to girls with simple social ability, such as being able to say "please" and "thank-you," "How are you?" "It's nice to meet you," "Yes, Ma'am," and the like.

Spend some time and effort teaching your daughter some simple rules of etiquette. Teach her to make simple introductions: "This is my friend Molly; Molly, this is my mother," "My name is Matilda; who are you?" Take her through each step of protocol and rehearse it a number of times. It isn't that hard, and she will actually like the feeling of doing something so simple with such profound effect. Extend your manners coaching to telephone answering and message taking, meeting strangers (children and adults) and visitors at the door, greetings, and salutations. Teach her to shake hands and grip firmly. Teach her to look into the eyes of the person she's speaking to. Teach her to respond when someone asks her a question.

These simple habits put your girl into a great social position! You do her a big favor by showing her how these graces are executed.

Express Anger Effectively

Anger is a tricky subject for girls. Most girls associate anger with violence, and violence is something girls just don't commonly engage in. It destroys the sense of connection and community they so carefully compose. So what is your daughter supposed to do with anger? Girls typically resort to what we know as "cattiness" when they're angry, because they have no acceptable means of quickly and effectively venting all the anger that rises in them. After the age of five or so, they'll do almost anything to avoid an outright burst of anger.

The difficulty here is that to teach girls to express anger runs counter to their own serenity-preserving instincts. To a girl, this hideous feeling just can't be shown! From our perspective, such instincts are highly irrational, but to a girl they make perfect sense.

Let's focus on three ways to develop your girl's ability to deal with anger around her.

1. Give her an "anger vocabulary"
2. Spot early anger signals
3. Encourage overall forthright expression

Give Her an "Anger Vocabulary"

You know how frustrating it can be to have anger welling up in you with no place to go. You feel like your head is going to blow! That feeling of uncontrollable fury rarely happens immediately; it usually occurs after talking has failed to relieve an anger-causing situation. Now think of your daughter: Her vocabulary makes yours look like Webster's, so should it be any surprise that she cannot express her anger well verbally? She just doesn't have the words to fix problems or allay frustration.

It makes perfect sense that, should you teach your daughter new words, she would more capably express what she feels, thus preventing or alleviating anger. Here is a brief menu of phrases that she might find helpful in explaining her feelings:

> You won't cooperate
> You're a hypocrite
> I feel frustrated
> I feel worried
> I feel disappointed
> I feel irritated
> I feel annoyed
> I feel hurt
> I feel jealous
> I feel aggravated
> I feel sad
> I was lied to
> I was left out
> I was ignored
> I was cheated

I was afraid
I was embarrassed

Ask your daughter if she knows what these phrases mean. If not, explain them in terms she can grasp, then ask her to repeat what they mean. Please note that our point is to build her ability to communicate so anger and ugly outbursts can be avoided or made more intelligible. Your daughter's angry outbursts, like yours, usually only happen following a string of unsuccessful or frustrating attempts to communicate. In other words, nobody really wants to blow up. In some sense an explosion is a failure. Those outbursts only serve the purpose of creating action when words won't. We should help make the words work.

Spot Early Anger Signals

We've all seen the little peanut who throws a tantrum in the grocery store, shouting, foot stomping, sobbing. It's a classic picture—one that should not be allowed.

That of course is when they are young. As they get older, say age five and up, you can begin the process of talking them through those tantrums. (By the way, if they continue to tantrum past the age of five, you better step in heavily with either a firmer approach or outside expertise. There is no reason for normal children past the age of five to have tantrums.) When your girl is visibly angry, take the opportunity to begin asking her questions. Draw her out on those matters that are causing her anger, and provide her a sounding board to talk it over. Again recall that her natural tendency is to find a way to discuss it. If you are there with the right platform at the right time, you can be a valuable asset for her. But *you* have to show up, and *you* have to offer yourself.

Encourage Overall Forthright Expression

As your daughter grows older, you can initiate the habit of general expressiveness as a means to vent anger. Learning to express herself in open and direct ways will be useful in many areas of her life, but venting anger appropriately is particularly useful. Girls need to be raised in an environment that allows for privately and verbally expressing fondness, repulsion, excitement, criticism, and other thoughts and sentiments. They need to be raised around people committed to not letting the sun go down on their anger. They need to be raised in an atmosphere that encourages rather than punishes expressions of honesty, accepts critical opinions without condemnation, and allows respectful questioning of authority when the authority is unreasonable.

What matters most in developing this kind of atmosphere is that these expressions be allowed to unfold in a private, one-on-one place. Remember that your daughter has learned how to deal with you. She has in her own head a set of rules she follows when she's in your presence: *Don't tell Dad he's a know-it-all or he'll kill me,* or *Mom always lectures me after dinner, so just stay quiet and it will end soon,* and so on. Your girl most likely feels that to violate those "rules" will bring forth some sort of Armageddon. Expect her to observe some minimal set of rules when you're around her publicly.

Privately, you can disable these rules and become a "safe" person to her. You must communicate to her that all the rules she knows to be true of you are off, and for the duration of your conversation she is free to speak what's on her mind, and you will listen uncritically, without blowing up. If she trusts you enough, she will talk. Building this trust sometimes takes years, especially if you begin when your daughter is older than ten, so set your expectations on "patient," and begin.

Express Opinions Clearly

Having an opinion and expressing it are two different matters. Let's assume for now that inside your girl is a burgeoning repository of opinions fit for expression. What can you do to encourage voicing those opinions?

How opinions are expressed is culture bound. Some cultures value stating opinions no matter how volatile or unpopular. These cultures reward people for sharing their divergent views. Other cultures disavow opinions that sway from accepted standards. These cultures intimidate or silence those too opinionated. The reasons for both extremes are complex, but all are based on a belief that opinions are powerful and need to be handled with care.

Families similarly vary in their view of how to express opinions. However, girls need to become skilled in expressing themselves, asking for what they need, and saying what they mean. This means that whatever has been your past family culture with regard to expressing opinions, now is the time to open up and grant your daughter freedom to speak her mind.

You may encounter problems. First of all, there's mounting evidence that shyness is a genetically inherited trait. Some kids are just naturally more quiet than others. They require additional encouragement in expressing themselves. Reward their attempts to communicate by letting them know their thoughts are valuable and welcome.

Second, girls are sharp-witted about discomfort. Most 1990s American homes are places where expressing strong opinions creates the sort of discomfort girls flee. The sole antidote is to find ways to remove the perceived threat created by expressing an opinion. It is not easy. However, like many other aspects of raising winning girls, it is most easily achieved by making something difficult into something matter-of-fact.

Girls don't know being opinionated is risky until someone teaches them. In exactly the same way, girls don't know being opinionated is fun until someone tells them! In short, you can make this frightening, or you can make this fun! Ask her what she thinks about anything—newspaper headlines, hot issues at school, actions of friends, family decisions that need to be made. Virtually any topic is a golden chance to press her into expressing preferences. Make it a point to ask for an opinion five times a day. Your interest in her opinion will eventually convince her of the utter value of her ideas. That's a good thing for her to learn.

Do not under any circumstances ridicule her ideas. Her ideas may often be immature and ridiculous, but you must fashion an outward attitude of rapt interest and credibility even when the ideas are crazy. The more you press, the more she'll express. Whether the ideas are right or wrong is not the point. The point is to lay the proper groundwork for this sort of talking to emerge. And, as a matter of good taste and fair play, discourage her from making disparaging remarks about others when they express themselves.

As you practice communication, your daughter's opinions will emerge. Encourage her to express them with as much clarity as she can muster, with respect for those she's speaking with, while attempting to be constructive and not merely complaining. No matter how awkward it may feel, demonstrate how to avoid interruptions, take turns in sharing opinions, and respectfully focus on what opinions others offer. Keep these lessons brief and concrete, using real-life examples as often as possible.

Express Self-Satisfaction Appropriately

Here's another gleaming side on the self-expression cube. Child psychologists have repeatedly observed a general reluctance among girls to take responsibility for good things happening in their lives. Isn't this odd? Girls credit good things in their life to luck, other people just being nice, no boys around to compete with, and so on. They just can't think *they're* great (*I got an A because I worked hard and earned it, My mom is nice because I do my best to listen to her and do as she says, My room is nice because I work hard to make it look cool*).

In addition to some of the antidotes for external locus of control mentioned in chapter 8, we offer the following prescription. First, listen carefully to your daughter speak, taking note of those times when she repels responsibility for something she's done that's good. Don't say anything the first few times you hear it; just keep a stealthy ear open and hear how often it occurs.

Then, apply a gentle word. When you hear her deflect something good she should own, simply and gently encourage her to claim "It was me." We've done this with many girls many times, and a consistent first reaction is a taut, embarrassed giggle. To say "I was good" is somehow forbidden. You need to assure your girl of the rightness of assuming responsibility for doing good things. It is not boasting. Make her rub up against some earned self-satisfaction.

Ask for What You Want

In our "Raising Winners" seminar we pose the question, What were you not taught as a child that you wish you had been taught? This question always brings lots of ideas. The leading comment among women is, "I was never taught to just ask for what I want." Not asking for what you want must be some form of female epidemic, for many women suffer from it.

After some discussion, we've concluded that this problem really begins to rear up at around the age of nine. Prior to that time, girls are quite able and willing to ask for what they want and say what they mean. At about nine, however, girls enter that peculiar stage when they become self-conscious. All sorts of changes sweep in at that time. Saying what they want is not typical of girls at this age. What is typical? Hemming and hawing, waffling and wavering, second-guessing and stalling! Even their firmest decisions are shot through with subterfuge and fear. What are typical are things that drive pragmatic and mature adults to the brink!

Thankfully, all you need to do to get them to ask for things directly is ask for it directly! In many ways this is related to decisiveness. Many young kids don't have an adult expecting them to ask for what they want, thus they don't learn that asking is good. In fact, understanding the psychology of girls leads us to think that perhaps they see forthrightness as a violation of one of their social codes. Girls don't break those! Your daughter makes her preferences known. She needn't try to please you or think she can gain favor through any means other than saying what she means and directly asking for what she wants.

Stand Up for Yourself

We want our girls to be tough enough to handle any situation. We also want our girls to be able to speak up on their own behalf, kindly, but firmly if push comes to shove. We also want our girls' actions to reflect their moral convictions, and they should be able to act forcefully on those principles should they need to. We must do what we can to prepare our girls for life's inevitable moments when all sense and civility break apart and they face the need to stand up for themselves.

We've learned much from those successful girls who consider it easy to stand up for themselves. These girls often say that standing up for themselves physically, socially, or emotionally is easy compared to the other more difficult things they've done in their lives—sports, competitions, piano recitals, learning to ride a bike.

Perhaps this lesson should be tried. Can you provide experiences for your girl that she would consider more difficult than standing up for herself? Which is harder for your girl, telling a group of girls she doesn't want to cheat on a test or learning karate? Which is harder, hiking with a backpack for a week in the summer or telling her teacher she has a different view on a questionable subject? What's hard to her is only a comparison to the hardest things she's ever done. Building backbone might in the long run best be accomplished by creating a physically demanding comparison experience whereby your girl can naturally conclude, "Standing up for myself is *nothing* compared to what I've done." That experience could be role-playing a backbone-building situation at home, saying no! to someone in a live situation, or conquering an enormous physical challenge. If she fails to make the connection between the difficulties she's known and the relative ease of standing up for herself, you can make the connection for her!

Ask Productive Questions

It's a common observation among those considered great conversationalists that they don't really converse much. Most will freely admit that rather than talking, they just ask questions. People on the other end of the conversation respond to the inquiries and leave feeling that the other person really understood them and was a great conversationalist. The same trick holds true with professional counselors who, though they say very little, are thought to be warm, accepting, and altogether understanding! Asking questions is a clever key to use to unlock girls.

There are closed questions and open questions. Closed questions are those that lead to yes or no answers. Examples of these might be, "Do you like beets?" "Are you doing well in school?" or "Can I count on you in the future?" They're considered closed because they request a simple yes or no answer. These questions can be conversational dead ends.

Open questions ask for more information. Examples include, "How do you think beets taste?" "What's school like?" or "How reliable are you?" You cannot easily answer questions posed in this form with a simple yes or no, hence their unique strength to draw girls into conversation.

We offer a strong warning against using "why" questions. "Why" questions will confuse your girl. When confused in conversations, girls typically retreat. On the surface that retreat looks like guilt or insubordination, which usually prompts more questions from us, which go further into nowhere. Avoid why questions.

The following types of questions can help you converse with your girl. These are all highly effective "stems," which when applied to the beginning of questions open conversations:

> How can you . . . ?
> What would be better . . . ?
> How can I . . . ?

Tell me about . . . ?
If . . . , then . . . ?
How do you . . . ?
What are some . . . ?

It may require some private practice on your part, but with some effort these question stems will become automatic. If all else fails, use a conversational bridge. When she stops talking, simply interject "and?" and wait. She will talk on. It works very well. Try it.

As these become a natural part of your conversational armament, you will find wide and friendly talks opening up. You will quickly reach a level of insight into your girl that you've never experienced before.

Talk with Her

Little girls gravitate to women for conversation. The attraction is natural and obvious. But fathers bring novel influences to their girls. Through simple conversations with fathers girls can learn a male sense of humor, decisiveness, analytical ability, male-style compassion, a sense of authority, security, expectations about how they ought to be treated by men, and a work ethic. Girls were meant to communicate effectively with men, so building a verbal bridge should be a priority.

But we recently encountered a disturbing study. Fathers were asked to rate how much time they spend a day speaking with their kids. The average reported was about twenty minutes per day. Then, the children were equipped with tape recorders to monitor how much father-to-child conversation actually took place. The average was thirty-seven *seconds* per day! No comment required.

Fathers, not only should you communicate more with your girl, but she wants to communicate more with you. Cross-gender talk to little girls is a jungle of surprises. The guidance your spouse offers can be your compass. Seek her input and clarification. Practice using the lingo your daughter uses, as this rapidly builds rapport. Look at her carefully as you speak; girls love that. And above all else, sit close to her, face-to-face, and make deliberate intermittent physical contact. We cannot begin to express the power such contact has on a little girl. It's equal in force to a hug and does miracles to reinforce the conversations you'll have.

As a man, you needn't do girltalk; you can talk to her any way you please and she'll soak it up. But remember, your girl is used to your previous habits. It may take her a while to become adjusted to your expressing interest in her, much less going out of your way to create rapport. She'll warm to it quickly, though. One of our *Girls!* Team members described her conversations with Dad as giving her that "Christmas morning feeling!"

Le Mot Juste

As writers we struggle and dig to find those elusive words that will make our message unforgettable. Though we'd like to say it's dictionaries and thesauruses that provide the tweak, it usually comes from comic books, cereal boxes, or loud, jazzy music! But oh, when you find just the right word— ooooh, it feels nice! As wordsmiths, we live for that word, *le mot juste!*

There's absolutely no need for such inspiration when talking with girls. Girls don't require just the right words, they just require words. Lavish words on your girl and watch her rise to her feet in excitement! Nothing satisfies quite the way a deep and meaningful conversation can.

Physical Play and Sports

If you ever want kids to open up quickly in a conversation, ask to see their scars. All kids have at least a cut or bruise on the mend, and with some small effort you can find a scar on any child. A wide swath of personal history is recorded in each nick. And they love to tell about it. Take for example a group of girls I (Bill) sat with one warm summer morning. One of these young women opened the bidding by complaining about a grotesque scab on her elbow. Something about her dog dragging her around. Then in chimed the others with a progression of stories building in a crescendo of drama and blood. The winner of course was I, who complained of being severed at birth from my mother, leaving behind a huge, ugly scar (my belly button, which I refused to show). They all laughed and spent the next few minutes picking around their grandest scar of all!

We're loath to let our little girls get too banged up. But don't you agree that there is something appealing about hardy little girls? We certainly aren't interested in raising roller derby queens, but most of us aren't opposed, at least in principle, to helping our girls become durable. In our culture durability is most easily taught through physical play and sports.

Learning through Sports

Our society is sports-obsessed. Kathi and I are asked countless questions about the health of being involved in sports. We still feel that sports and physical challenge are good and need to be embraced by everyone. Girls, no matter how physically fit (or not), need some sort of physical outlet to be healthy and normal. Sports challenges are demanding and help create physical coordination, heightened concentration, aerobic fitness, stress relief, and other benefits. Girls raised in the absence of good, hard, vigorous physical activity are stunted in many ways, not to mention unprepared for the physical rigors of life.

We would like to suggest that there are five uniformly tough lessons to teach your daughter through sports. We know of no other way to nicely teach these skills. Each is unique and prerequisite for teaching her the constructive side of struggling. These lessons require scrapes with real life, but sensible scrapes for a specific purpose.

1. Get in the game and play hard
2. Be willing and able to defend yourself
3. Deal with pain and losing
4. Gain stamina
5. Win and have fun

Get in the Game and Play Hard

The best lessons sports offer are learned through simple participation. Just help your girl get involved physically with some organized sport or game. Though our society has made enormous strides in including girls in competitive sports, we still tend to think of sports and games as boy stuff. No! In fact, tough game situations form some of the most enduring memories your daughter can ever have. Do you remember some of your best games?

Several members of our *Girls!* Team were avowed tomboys. They've told us one great story after another of being left out by the boys, only to practice and practice and whip them at a later time. This story is pure Americana. And most girls have their own version.

Don't permit your girl to miss this slice of life. Sports and games provide a means to learn body and attitude control and serve as a test tube to try out skills and social abilities they can use elsewhere. Since girls were meant to be on teams in the first place (families), participation should be natural. No matter what her skill or lack of, encouraging your daughter's participation in physical events is an important part of your parental responsibility.

Some girls don't like physical contact or activity. You need to encourage it anyway; it's that important. In our "Raising Winners" seminar, we suggest that the health of your relationship with your girl is proportional to the number of carpet burns on your elbows! Get down on the ground and take her along! How often do we actually climb down off our restful perch atop the holy couch and play physically? Not often enough. Girls like some physical playfulness, and we need to oblige that preference often, daily if you like. Light periodic rough-housing is an undeniable form of "I love you!" Think this is untrue? Try it. Get physical!

There's no need to force yourself overnight to become a rough-houser. If you're like 99 percent of all other parents, such active play with your girl may be foreign. We overprotect these darlings. You will find your daughter more than up to the challenge and will in fact discover that her appetite for fun contact is insatiable. She's much tougher than she thinks. There are dozens of sports your daughter can try, ranging from simple tumbling to basketball, ballet, bike riding or racing, roller skating, gymnastics, marksmanship with guns, swimming, and on and on. Your local school, YMCA, or community center will have extensive lists of activities they offer. Look them over and decide on something you can do together. It is a vital part of her growth.

Be Willing and Able to Defend Yourself

I (Bill) remember a little girl I worked with on the issue of toughness. The common counseling maneuver to her problem, dealing with bullies, was to build her self-esteem and help her rise above the rabble. She had tried thinking herself above her challengers, talking to them, running away, reasoning, all to no avail. I came to think a boxer's right hook would serve her best! For a number of sessions we worked on building her fearlessness and having some backbone. She visited me on subsequent weeks with stories about what she was learning.

I'll never forget this sawed-off little firecracker strolling into my office one afternoon like John Wayne, telling me she had something to show me. "Stand up, Mr. Beausay," she commanded. I felt as though I shouldn't cross this lass, so I did. She calmly walked toward me, eyes glaring at my gut. Then without warning she planted her fist squarely into my blubber! I yelped and reeled backward, choking with laughter! Case closed! We spent that session discussing when to use her newfound fists and when to be kind and gentle!

Physical self-defense is not a big deal to little girls, for most of them are stronger and faster than boys of their age. Self-defense, however, becomes critical as your girl grows and potential threats to her person increase. Physically aware girls are better able to protect themselves and are thus safer than those with no body awareness. This is a good reason to push your girl to get active in some physical challenge. Self-defense and sports are nicely intermingled in martial arts, but these might require more involvement than your girl wishes to have. If so, encourage her to strengthen herself physically and learn some simple self-defense moves.

We certainly don't advocate violent solutions to problems, but we don't preclude them either. Properly preparing your daughter for life includes getting her in shape for ugly situations. Life won't spare her transient trouble. Therefore, we advocate helping your daughter get used to aggressive physical action. This comes by getting her used to her own body, how it moves, how it struggles when pressed, and how to use it forcefully. It's easy. Lightly wrestle with her. Make certain that she learns to resist your moves, and in simple ways teach her how to make proactive moves to get you before you get her. We know this sounds like wrestlemania, and to some degree it is. In a gentle, playful way you want your daughter to fight back physically, not to lay down the struggle and yield too quickly. You want her to stand and fight, even when facing considerable odds! For one day she may face someone who wishes to do her personal harm.

Deal with Pain and Losing

We heard a great story of a successful coach of girls' soccer, who gave some profound and distinctly masculine advice to his new team. He started by saying he expected them to have a good time but he had one rule that he absolutely would not bend: no crying! He made it clear that there were only three conditions under which the girls were allowed to cry: (1) their mother had died, (2) a bone was sticking out of their skin, or (3) they were giving birth to a baby. The girls all laughed but learned the ominous reality that soccer is painful.

Life is painful too. We try to shield that fact from our girls. Because of our passion and high hopes, we lean steeply toward cautious protection rather than healthy exposure. We see most physical challenge as overexposure and regularly detour our girls past the perceived danger or difficulty. We've forgotten the simple lesson that the fight makes us strong.

One member of our *Girls!* Team succinctly stated, "Anyway, it may sound strange, but dealing with pain as a girl made me a tough, strong, I believe better, adult. We certainly don't want to inflict pain on our kids, but I believe it can be a strong character builder to shape leaders of the future." We must let our daughters learn the unique lessons pain teaches and allow them to suffer decisive losses.

Pain

Most girls are *afraid* of pain. Think about that. Not only does it hurt, but also they fear the pain ahead of time. You can almost always bet that whenever a girl is hesitant to try some daring or novel thing, it is because of her fear of pain. Some girls never outgrow it. Pain makes cowards of many of us. There is no way to shield your daughter from physical pain. The only thing you can do is teach her not to fear pain so much that she stops trying new and interesting things.

How? By familiarizing her with pain. Do you remember your first bee sting? You were sure you'd die. As children we interpret all pain as life ending. It is only with time that we learn that pain never brings death (if it did you'd be dead and wouldn't know it) and that pain is, in fact, no big deal. But how do we act when our girls get hurt? Most of us just turn freaky and act in the most juvenile and ridiculous ways! Our girls see that, and taking the cue from us, believe that whatever they are feeling will kill them. There is a mighty fine line between compassion and blathering overreaction.

Don't let yourself be so shook up about pain. Deliberately let your girl suffer a little pain. The only sane way for that to happen is to have her play hard in some physical game or sport. Not long ago our family participated in a unique event: Bill ran a marathon, and the kids ran in an adjoining one-mile run. The kids were in good shape, but a mile run pushed them. They all did fine, but what would you expect a child just forced to run one mile to complain of? Right: sore legs.

Now consider this. There is no way a bee sting could compare to the pain of unprepared legs having just run one mile. But the kids were smiling! They got ribbons and drinks! The pain was a celebrated mark of achievement and victory! I dare say that a bee sting would have transformed them all into anaphylactic hysterics! Pain, you see, is not the issue; it's how the pain is interpreted that matters. Interpret it as death, and they act like they're dying. Interpret it as natural, and they ignore it.

One of the most physically challenging sports events in the world is the Iditarod Trail Sled Dog Race. It's held annually and traverses 1,150 miles of isolated Alaskan wilderness. It's raced over approximately eleven days of constant discomfort: incessant sub-zero weather, frostbite, hours of icy silence and loneliness, fear of wild animals, dangerous terrain, relentless wind, and scores of minor troubles. Men have died racing in this treacherous, decades-old event. This is no place for wusses.

In 1985 history was made when the Iditarod was won by a woman, Libby Riddles. Libby Riddles won by being both the best and most tenacious, as Burt Bomhoff, a leading competitor, describes:

> She didn't baby her dogs, though, or herself. Once I stopped with several other drivers to rest and warm up in a lodge alongside the trail. Libby drove up, and her dogs wanted to stop. She told them no in a language they could understand. Real colorful language. And off they went. I had to admire her for that. We were all relaxing and getting warm, but she never came in. She just told those dogs to keep moving down the trail.[10]

Later Bomhoff was able to offer his respects . . . as Libby waited for him at the finish line.

In the years since Libby Riddles first won the Iditarod, more women than men have been victors in that race! Don't let pain steal your girl's life. Teach her to master it at a young age, and a world of adventure and excitement opens to her!

Losing

It always bugs us a little bit to hear children make excuses for losses. It's as if they just cannot bring themselves to admit that someone else is better than they (gee, I wonder where they learn that?). After speaking with scores of kids who are what we call winners, we offer some strong suggestions with regard to losing.

Sports are supposed to teach life lessons. *Let them.* One of the lessons frequently lost on young athletes is that losing means something. It means that we can get better. It means that other people worked harder and deserved what they earned. It means that there are avenues to excellence we didn't know about, avenues on which to continue our journey toward being our very best. It can also mean that others are simply superior. And that's all right.

These lessons are good and they aren't learned by some obscure psychological osmosis. They are learned over and over through countless losses and reevaluations, through countless tears of frustration and determination, through hours of practice and anticipation, through being tough on yourself. This really is the grit of life, the place of life champions; and it's all first motivated by stinging defeat.

Let defeat knock your girl down and sting her. Then pick her up, dust her off, and help her back to the drawing board. That's life, and God didn't make a more perfect teacher.

Gain Stamina

Girls won't quit a difficult endeavor unless permitted, nor move forward unless encouraged. You can permit or encourage. Never calling it quits is called "stamina," and moving forward after a setback is called "a second wind." Make these two practices the sword and shield of your winning girl.

One of the real joys of working with girls in the area of physical play and sports is that results are rapid. Most of the other areas we've discussed (building heart, brains, spirit) take time to develop and evaluate. Whether or not you've done the right thing needs to wait to be decided, sometimes for years. Sports endeavors provide feedback with cold immediacy. There are no credible equivocations or excuses. It's clinical: She played and won or played and lost.

For parents who prefer to feather life just a bit for their

girl, this reality of sports will seem too intense. It is not. We know this suggestion will sound Spartan, but girls raised on a diet of difficulty gain stamina. It is the only way to build stamina. One of the truly great things about sports is that stamina is taught automatically. All you must do as a parent is promote participation and cheerlead.

Oh, and one more thing: Don't let her quit! She will certainly beg and fuss about quitting. That's normal. When you were little you wanted to quit too. If you think quitting is in her long-term best interest, then allow it. But if you truly believe that self-discipline must be learned, then make her go to practice when she's tired, make her practice on her own periodically, and don't pamper and placate.

A girl makes an important discovery when she starts seizing control of her life. She suddenly discovers what we adults call the "comfort zone." In essence she discovers that she can make choices that lead to places of safety and comfort. Not being a dummy, she finds out what her comfort level is and seeks it routinely.

But there is one enormous problem: Her comfort zone (and ours) is always set way too easy for her own good, and quickly entombs her. Her preset comfort zone is not the place of happiness or achievement; it is merely a place of comfort. Gently push her out of her comfort zone. Make her stretch herself ever so slightly. Always try to help her squeeze just a little more out of herself. Just a little bit more discomfort, just a little longer, just a little bit harder, and so on.

The sports crossover here is obvious and easy. To be athletic is by definition to strive for something greater. She will not be a born soccer player; she will have to stretch uncomfortably and learn. She will not be born knowing how to jump rope; she will have to stretch and learn. She will not be born knowing how to do karate; she will have to stretch, fight, suffer pain and humiliation, and learn. Sports and physical participation at any level will make your daughter spring out of her comfort zone. Make sure to allow that to happen.

Win and Have Fun

A woman we know told a great story about a game she and a small group of girls used to play against the boys. The girls would ride their bikes up and down a driveway, and the boys would sit along the edges of the concrete and push their skateboards into the path of the onrushing bikes. If the boys knocked the girls off the bikes, the boys won, and if the girls stayed on their bikes, the girls won. We laughed to ourselves as she recounted with glee that *the boys never won!* She had that wild-eyed, winner's sparkle about her! Winning that battle was serious, and victory was very sweet, memorable enough to be recalled thirty years later!

Yes, it's good to win. We should teach our girls that winning is getting what you want regardless of the effort needed. It's a high achievement to get where you want to go and to accomplish what you wish for. Those achievements hit a satisfying spot in our lives. We should allow our girls to know that *winning means earning,* and that's good and fun.

Is winning overemphasized? No, not by most of the parents we know. There are exceptions, of course, but for the most part parents are good about balancing winning as a goal with the reality that it doesn't happen all the time. In fact, it may be that winning is being *underemphasized,* especially for our girls. In our opinion underemphasizing winning just might pose a greater threat to the future of your daughter than overemphasizing it.

For a complex array of reasons, parents don't like to talk about winning too much, especially to their girls. Spotlighting winning runs counter to the prevailing breezes of social fairness, accommodation, cultural sensitivity, and the rest. It implies that some are better than others and that we can actually have superiority over others. Even though all this is true, it's not cool for parents to say it.

Whether you're a gifted athlete or just a hard worker the bottom line is the same: Anyone can improve himself or herself. It's all right to stretch and be your best. Improving yourself requires great amounts of effort, and if that means you end up being better than others, that's fine. Let's speak openly about being the best: Striving to be the best is a noble, difficult thing.

Take the simple steps of encouraging your daughter to be her physical best and urging her to try to win in whatever she's doing. That will make her stretch. The trick, if there is any, is to make losing as valued as winning. No girl likes to lose, no matter how much parental salve is spread, but losing is a tool to motivate more improvement. Use it to build in her the habit of pursuing personal excellence regardless of the final outcome. In other words, stretch to win, but should you fail, regroup, rethink, and try again.

Make this process fun! Winning and losing can be great experiences. But they can both be painful and meaningless unless you as a parent step back and get a full perspective on what winning and losing is all about. Laugh with the winners, cheer up the losers, and be ever grateful and thankful that you can run and jump and play! Sports are to be fun. Play them that way, but as you smile, shoot high to win!

A Special Note to Those with No Physical Ability

There is a very small group of girls who cannot participate in sports in any way. To parents of these girls let us offer some encouragement. Keep trying. If your daughter can move, she can participate in something. Just be alert for opportunities, and be prepared to create some team or club yourself if need be. The benefits are much more than physical. Camaraderie, teamwork, and the joy of meeting a challenge are wonderful benefits gained by those who play chess, do computer simulations, or compete in tag-team knitting!

The activity itself is irrelevant. *What is relevant is participation.* Find ways to help your child plug in with others in some focused team effort no matter how ridiculous or frivolous it may appear to be on the surface.

Part 4

*Raising Girls
to a
Higher Plateau
of Accomplishment*

11

The Magic of Mastery

Practice yourself, for heaven's sake, in little things;
and thence proceed to greater.

Epictetus

What you are is God's gift to you;
What you make of yourself is your gift to God.

Anonymous

I never did anything worth doing by accident nor did
any of my inventions come by accident. They came by
work.

Thomas Edison

We need to spend a few moments doing something
controversial. We must build a case against a sacred cow called
"self-esteem." You've probably heard of the importance of
building self-esteem, and that's the reason we feel impelled
to make this assault. Let us set the record straight.

We get a strong negative reaction whenever we hear the term *self-esteem*. Over the last twenty years it has come to mean accepting and liking yourself whether or not you are acceptable or likable. Having self-esteem implies thinking you're okay irrespective of any standards of excellence. We don't think this view is very good and in good conscience cannot encourage you to think it is. We need to take a fresh look at the whole concept of self-esteem and redefine it.

A Brief History of *Self-Esteem*

Building a child's self-esteem has been a hot issue for years. The topic has found its way into most child-related functions. Find a public school that doesn't include building self-esteem as a major part of its mission. Find a parent who hasn't heard of its importance. Find a childrearing text that doesn't mention it. Find a government program that doesn't harp on it. *Self-esteem* is a dynamic buzzword that springs effortlessly off the lips of all who want good things for kids. Wanting our kids to have self-esteem is very noble. As with all noble efforts, it pays us to periodically conduct a reality check. What are we trying to accomplish in building a child's self-esteem? Is self-esteem the end or the means? If we deem self-esteem the end, what methods have we chosen to attain it, and are they the best? Are there better means to get where we want to go?

We've passed a critical era in the ongoing mobilization of self-esteem. We've gone beyond the point of asking ourselves if self-esteem (as it is commonly defined) is *right* to concluding that it is necessary: Kids must esteem themselves to get ahead. We've mistakenly made a quaint idea—loving yourself is good—into an institutionalized necessity. This shift in thinking has been costly, for by assuming that self-esteem is right, we've drifted far away from what we intended to create in our kids.

What were we trying to accomplish by this emphasis on self-esteem in the first place? I (Bill) was always told that you cannot love others or perform adequately until you love yourself. Maybe you heard that too. We were taught that self-love (or at least self-acceptance) formed the basis of reaching full personal potential. "If we just *feel good about ourselves,* then we can yatta datta datta . . ." has been the party line of social reformers for years, and it's wrong. Feeling good about yourself is not the sole criterion for happiness in life.

On what grounds do we conclude this? Because the world is bursting with people who think little of themselves yet are loving parents, productive and constructive members of society, genuinely great folks! They're talented and creative and clearly in control of themselves and their abilities. They in fact seem perplexed when you question them about their self-esteem, not seeming to be much aware of themselves in the ongoing flow of life. People such as these provide clear evidence that loving yourself, or being aware of loving yourself, is unrelated to actually performing well with the talents and abilities you were born with.

This observation has led us to a radical proposal: Maybe we can do without self-esteem. Maybe we can even do without self-love! Was that the sound of jaws dropping we just heard? Let's examine this idea some more.

Let yourself wonder what life would be like if suddenly self-esteem disappeared off the face of the planet. To those staunchly defending self-esteem as the cornerstone of good mental health, such a disappearance would appear catastrophic.

But it is distinctly possible that rather than developing into heartless, mentally ill monsters, we all might improve. Rather than dumping energy and effort into making ourselves feel good about ourselves, we would do other things. It's hard to predict exactly what, but on the list might be such things as focusing on others, deriving more satisfaction from extending our talents than celebrating those we already have, letting our love flourish beyond the mirror, and putting others ahead of ourself. Hmmm. A self-esteem-free society has some intriguing elements!

It *should* disturb us that a society of people ignoring themselves would be a better alternative than the one we have! Is it possible that our current preoccupation with building self-esteem without demanding performance is wrong? We think so.

The New Approach

Not long ago I had the opportunity to ask a small group of fifth graders what self-esteem was. They all looked at each other, then shrugging, told me they'd have to look it up in their D.A.R.E. book (D.A.R.E., Drug Abuse Resistance Education, is the government antidrug program for school children). After some more hesitation, one girl in the group said, "It's when you feel good about yourself and won't take drugs."

"Do you feel good about yourself?" I asked.

Silence and nervous glances.

One of the other girls said sheepishly, as if hers was the wrong answer, "We're not sure."

"Well, how do you know if you like yourselves?" I asked.

Twitching and nervous giggles.

"I guess we just don't know," was all they could say.

This conversation illustrates an important point. We have a multimillion-dollar government program in place to help children stay drug free. This program is based ultimately on kids feeling good about themselves so they will make sound choices. But kids don't know how they feel about themselves! Even if these little girls could have told me what they thought of themselves, can we assume it would be any more genuine than answers memorized from some book? If we want our efforts to raise self-esteem to be any more potent than empty incantations, we need to look at building kids from kids' perspectives.

Years back when we began to focus on self-esteem, what we really wanted to accomplish was showing our kids that their lives had value. Teaching value continues to be a great goal. But talking about children's lives having value and demonstrating that value are two entirely different matters. We need to become more effective in showing girls their skills and talents and not just talking about them

But there's a problem in showing girls their own strengths. Girls are in the process of developing clear opinions about themselves, regardless of your input. Do they "like" themselves? That's an impossible question to answer. Prior to age six, they don't much know they exist. After age six, they spend a great deal of time comparing themselves to others. That's perfectly normal and will not ever change. This comparison, for better or worse, leads every girl to keep a private list of things about herself she wishes she could change. And she almost always underestimates herself. That's legendary!

We all seek ways to better ourselves. That's good. We need to keep growing and changing. What matters as far as our girls are concerned is learning how to do this well.

Here's the key: Girls only feel good about themselves if they have what they believe to be the power to improve or change themselves. That belief is the key to convincing her that her life has value. It is also a major key in balancing self-satisfaction (which is good) with self-absorption (which not only serves no purpose but may be detrimental).

Self-Respect through Mastery

Self-respect begins to form when a girl realizes she controls herself and can alter what she wishes. From a girl's perspective, self-respect means that your life is valuable and you can steer it, that you are talented and can change. What a great thing for a girl to learn! That definition of self-respect is so much more substantial than the "liking yourself" of self-esteem.

How do you build in your daughter this sort of self-respect and sense that she can control her own life? By teaching her to do things and to become very good at some of them. By making her capabilities demonstrable rather than simply teaching her to talk to herself about how great she is. This is called "building mastery" and plays a big role in forming your daughter's identity.

In many respects, this idea of mastery has infiltrated this whole book. We've encouraged you to build actual abilities in your daughter and haven't spent much time encouraging you to make her feel good about herself. Talent expressed and abilities publicly demonstrated are self-rewarding achievements. By being good, she can experience what we call "lifetime moments," those memories of specific successes she'll carry with her decades into the future. Those memories of success prove her ability and yield self-respect. The value of such memories cannot be measured.

"Trickle In" Psychology

Creating mastery in your daughter is similar to the economic principle we've come to know as "trickle-down" economics. In trickle-down economics, rather than give money to the needy, money or tax breaks are allocated to businesses to create more wealth, which creates a stronger economy, giving the poor a greater opportunity to get jobs and build a better life for themselves.

In "trickle-in" psychology, the same principle applies. Rather than our using empty praise to try to build in our girls inner strength, the girls are immersed in an atmosphere where they cannot help but gain some mastery or skill over something. This causes a sense of accomplishment and pride to trickle in, building a firm sense that they are valuable and good. This is a vastly superior way to build self-respect than the self-esteem way, which amounts to verbal welfare. It neither works well nor makes the recipient productive and satisfied.

Mastery builds naturally when your girl finds things she passionately loves to do and focuses on one or two to really hone. Finding and publicly displaying mastery in something specific is a bull's-eye method of developing all those fine things aimed for by the self-esteemies. What's best is that it fits naturally with so many of the directions and aspirations your girl longs for anyway. Not only is mastery fun, but it develops pride, a work ethic, the understanding of sacrifice, high inner standards of achievement, and a sense of true personal value. Yes, this has the warm ring of rightness to it!

Finding Something to Master

Before we delve into finding your daughter something to master, you should keep a few ideas pasted on the inside of your eyelids. First, for all of our discussion about shaping people, everyone has a core personality established, probably at conception. All personal growth is set against this natural background. As always we believe that girls can go much further than they think, but certain aspects of their personality are everpresent and may never change. We use the word *may* because miracle transformations in people happen every day, and we advocate believing everything about a person can change. It's an exciting way to live!

Second, your daughter's likes have probably already surprised, disappointed, angered, or embarrassed you. When I (Kathi) was ten I had dreams of someday being the lead majorette in the band. I was taking piano, violin, and tennis lessons and I begged my parents for baton lessons. They graciously conceded and dutifully deposited me each week in the driveway of the head majorette. During the next two years I practiced fervently, sustaining many bruises and bumps. My parents remained supportive despite the embarrassment they must have experienced as I dropped my baton repeatedly in view of the whole neighborhood. I was the only baton student who didn't seem to progress much and was not invited to competitions! However, I wasn't discouraged. Even with all the lumps on my head I was having fun! One day I realized that although twirling was enjoyable I would never lead the band. If my parents were elated or relieved they never let on. They gave me an ice bag and asked me to play them a tune on the piano.

Try to keep your ego out of the activity choices your daughter makes. Your job is simply to help her discover her own talents and to introduce her to activities that help her express them. Your passions are not hers, and attempting to push your interests onto her only delays her making her own good choices.

Third, make yourself excited about her excitement. I (Kathi) am not particularly interested in flutes, computers, and baseball, but my daughter is. Seeing her excited and interested on her own is gratifying. I appreciate and enjoy her talents even if I don't share her interests.

If you've taken seriously our suggestions up to this point in the book, we're certain you're trying to expose your girl to a wide pallet of experiences and opportunities. Mastery is as much an attitude as a skill, and your girl has the attitude naturally. She knows what she likes; encourage her to pursue what she really enjoys, and she'll build mastery almost completely on her own—as it should be!

The fairest thing you can do is open the world to your girl in the most hands-on way possible. Go to the library, read magazines, rent videos, find clubs, hear speakers, meet interesting people doing interesting things, ask other mothers what their girls are interested in. Widen the choices as far as you can.

Timing can be critical in presenting options. What your daughter hates today may be next week's obsession. What's hot today may be lame next week. In your own way, circulate ideas and don't permanently eliminate those ignored at first. As life's road bends and turns, keep a sharp eye out for her developing and emerging talents and gifts. Reintroduce old ideas as they become appropriate.

Don't let prevailing sex biases limit her choices, either. One of our *Girls!* Team members told a cute story about taking her twin daughters to female doctors. These included a pediatrician, dentist, orthodontist, optometrist, and obstetrician. The girls where shocked when later in their teen years they were attended by a *male* general practitioner. They came back to their mother and said, "He can't be a doctor, he's a MAN!" Both girls went on to become doctors.

Another of our *Girls!* Team members told us of her fascinating relationship with her dad, who helped her master "manly things," particularly mechanics: "My father fostered the confidence to try. He conveyed to me that I was a 'can-do' kind of person with few if any gender limitations. We worked side-by-side fixing cars, changing tires, mowing the grass, mixing cement, running electrical wires, roofing the house, and building a garage. He was patient and never condescending when mistakes were made. I did not realize how important his attitude was until I went to college and was surrounded by many women who seemed quite helpless. It seemed to me that this would hinder them in workplace competition. . . . It's funny now, but I really feel sorry for those girls. I believe that his confidence in me has been at the root of my overall survival and success.

"During one fix-it session, my dad was explaining to me that what he was doing would *eliminate* the problems with the boat motor. After thinking this through and assessing the situation, I replied, 'Well, that will be okay until the *eliminator* wears out!' My dad never cracked, and left my dignity intact, as well as my budding scientific thinking. It wasn't until much later that I learned what a belly laugh I'd provided for my parents."

Finding Her Talent

For those of you struggling with finding things your girl loves to do, allow us to suggest a clear way to narrow the focus. You will recall from chapter 6 our discussion of the seven types of intelligence. This would be an excellent place in which to apply that knowledge. The intelligences include musical, spatial, logical-mathematical, interpersonal, intrapersonal, linguistic, and bodily-kinesthetic intelligence.

Let this list swizzle your thinking. Musical mastery could be learning to play an instrument well, singing, or sound engineering (like using a digital synthesizer) skills. Spatial mastery could include drawing, painting, using computers, interior design (rearranging furniture), and the like. Logical-mathematical mastery could include games of logic like chess, using a computer, or perhaps advanced hobbies requiring science or engineering skills. Interpersonal mastery could include starting and belonging to clubs, selling things, entrepreneurial ventures, being the member of some team. Intrapersonal mastery would be difficult primarily because girls of this age aren't "into" themselves like an older person might be. If your daughter is a highly introverted child, do what you can to encourage her to stretch herself out into one of the other areas. Linguistic mastery could be honed through drama classes and plays, student politics, and many extracurricular clubs. Bodily-kinesthetic mastery could of course be found in sports, simple sleight-of-hand magic, and numerous outdoor pursuits.

These seven specific intelligences are present inside your daughter now, and no matter how uninterested she may seem, one or more of those intelligences is hers in abundance. With some gentle, focused exposure she'll race to it. We know this list is neither exhaustive nor fail proof. So use it as a prompt, a fuse, or a pry bar!

Don't give up. Be supportive of your girl when she tests herself. We have worked with so many girls who looked for all the world like they would never come out of their shells, who develop interests and then suddenly begin to flourish! The only commonality we can find in these cases is parents who refused to give up the stroking, suggesting, cheerleading, cajoling, and drawing out. She'll choose something; just stay with her!

If she's still finding it difficult to settle on something to master, another problem may be brewing. We've discussed the reality that to some extent your girl has a natural tendency to deny her own talent. What this means from a practical side is that she will tend to underestimate her talent. It's interesting how girls relate to their own talents. Many girls participate in events to *ratify* their talents rather than *improve* them. They try out different skills for the purpose of seeing how their skills fit in rather than pushing their skills to a higher level.

Ratifying and improving are clearly different, the first comparative, the second competitive. Because many girls don't believe enough in their own skill, they attempt new things with fear. They don't feel themselves able to stand up to any significant challenge. They shrivel and quit at the first sign of someone else's superiority. Other girls are the opposite. Not only do they feel competent, but they are also anxious to test themselves and get better—and be better than others. These girls can be found in all pursuits.

Which is better? The best spot is, as usual, a mix of the two. Here are some general recommendations for finding the right blend. If your daughter is less than eight or nine, don't bother making her focus. Let her enjoy the smorgasbord of interesting things life has to offer. After that age, though, it is appropriate to encourage her to begin to get good at a few things, if she hasn't already done so by herself. We make this suggestion because every girl we've ever known leans toward an area of mastery around this age. It's as if genetics had endowed them with the urge to focus and be good. It makes sense to stay with this natural drift and make the way clear for it to emerge.

If your girl doesn't select an area of mastery on her own, help her along some. The best way is to recruit some of her friends involved in doing activities similar to what she appears to enjoy. Few girls at this age are generalists, and most are beginning to find their niches, so find "birds of a feather" and encourage friendships. Always include her in what you enjoy doing. If you don't have any hobbies or interests, get some (any wonder she hasn't any?). If all else fails and she just won't get any interests, then do the wise thing and back off. Some girls bloom late. Be patient, but continue to expose her to experiences that might interest her or develop some spark. It will happen. Persevere!

Natural Predators

This natural drive toward mastery has predators. There are normal tendencies in all girls that sabotage their best efforts. Be forewarned so you are not surprised but more importantly so you can preempt any weakly reasoned, radical move by your daughter to abandon a promising area of mastery.

Discouragement

The first predator is discouragement. Unlike the rest of your daughter's life, being good at something isn't easy nor is success in it guaranteed. Let's look at the life most girls lead. School? You can't lose; you can always get a G.E.D. Home life? Requires little real effort for most girls. Sports? Optional and easy. Jobs? The jobs we give our girls are easy and are for the most part guaranteed successes.

You just about cannot fail in America. You can't starve, there are food stamps; you can't be broke, there's government assistance; and you can't flunk out of school—without actually trying. There are plenty of jobs for those willing to work. Life is a cinch here compared to the rest of the world. Our girls think being good at something is as easy as snapping their fingers.

Those who pursue mastery are more often hounded by feelings of failure and self-doubt than feelings of success and control. If your daughter is unusually driven, then blasting through feelings of doubt should be easy. But most girls will be looking for more ease and some kind of guarantee that they will achieve their goal. Since no ease nor guarantee exists, it's up to you to help your daughter learn *optimism*.

How do you do that? Give your daughter brutal honesty, high expectations, and encouragement. One member of our *Girls!* Team tells how supportive parents and a tough teacher led her in mastering the piano: "There was a delicate balance in my family between expectations and praise. They counted on me working hard to become something and would not settle for lame attempts in anything from schoolwork to crafts. My parents let me choose the things I wanted to try. Once the goal was chosen, we were not permitted to simply let it fly with the wind. There had to be serious long-term effort given to accomplish whatever gift we wanted to develop.

"But was she strict (my piano teacher). I worked like a dog just to play right, and she was brutally honest. I kind of liked it that praise didn't flow as freely from her as from my parents. She always ended my lesson by playing something for me from her repertoire. I think it was the first time I really saw how hard it was to be truly excellent at something."

Frustration

Another predator of specific mastery is frustration. Girls have difficulty perceiving their own improvement. This leads to frustration and quitting. You need to be the one who creatively demonstrates progress before your daughter begins to question it. Look for ways to show that her achievement is far more advanced than she thinks. This will be a hard sell because—remember—girls cannot see themselves very well. But stay with her and remain vigilant and encouraging to her. Show her that her talent is unfolding at just the right pace. This helps build her confidence in her progress.

Girls as a general rule mentally metabolize confidence quickly. They munch through it like a bag of popcorn at a good movie. In other words, it doesn't last long, rarely long enough to help her persevere very far. Just accept that as the rule and prepare yourself to be her bottomless source of strength and vision.

Five Mastery Reminders

There are five things you can do to build a powerhouse of self-respect and performance excellence in your daughter.

1. Protect her good efforts
2. Learn to teach in "chunks"
3. Build pride in attacking the impossible
4. Use critic repellent
5. Let her teach you

Protect Her Good Efforts

We think one of the most awesome things parents can witness is their own girl doing something good, motivated by her own urges. I suppose that as parents we spend so much time shepherding that we fail to step back to enjoy what our lambs have become, to witness the good things that spring from within them. Their own initiative is a powerful, dare we say holy, thing. It should be protected and nurtured as if it were life itself.

Do what you can to help your children experience some victories in life, even if it means letting them win games, letting them receive change at the store, letting them get ahead in lines, and so on. Place them in the middle of the action of your life and let them experience simple wins. With your daughter, go one step more: Protect her efforts and tries at things. Do all you can to insure a success when she steps out and risks.

Learn to Teach in "Chunks"

We have learned from experience that what stops many girls from gaining mastery over some skill is an erroneous belief that they just couldn't achieve what they wish they could. To the contrary, we've found that with few exceptions, any girl can accomplish anything she wishes. She just needs to take the first few steps, get some success, and away she goes. How do we arrange that?

B. F. Skinner demonstrated that if you break down any behavior into simple steps, given enough time and the right reinforcers you could teach any organism to do practically anything. This idea is now known as "Chunking." In principle this sounds great, but in practice, especially with mastery and girls, it's even better!

Let's say your daughter really wishes to learn to dance. Most girls love to dance but quickly get self-conscious and hesitant to really boogie in public. Any girl can master dancing quickly if it's broken down into simple, easy, fun moves. The first "chunk" is moving your shoulder around. That's all you do for a while. Add to that rolling your eyes uncontrollably. Do both for a while. Then bang your feet back and forth on the floor. Do all three chunks for a while. Then occasionally snap your fingers. Get your daughter to try a few simple moves on her own, let her have some success, then look out! She'll learn the rest by herself and probably never forgive you for teaching her to dance so weirdly! (Okay, so we're geek dancers. We do have fun!)

You can break any task down into a series of simple movements that are *too* easy! Using chunking, your girl never has to feel intimidated in trying anything new! With your help, she can fearlessly try anything in a series of connected small chunks.

Speaking of fearlessly, . . .

Build Pride in Attacking the Impossible

What do you think it would be like to meet a girl who really thought she could do anything in the world she wanted—one who doesn't look at obstacles as insurmountable, never sees a challenge that doesn't look beatable, never feels a fear she isn't willing to conquer? Many of us might be just a little nervous about having our girl around someone like that, because such girls could be doing risky things that put themselves in danger. But a little of that fearlessness is all right.

Fearlessness is a psychological cornerstone of mastery. This is not a generic fearlessness that leads to bad choices and danger, but a fearlessness in one area—an ability to search, explore, and experiment in that area with reckless self-confidence. One of the beauties of building mastery over one specific skill is that as your girl mentally begins to "own" that area, she becomes comfortable taking risks there. She gains a specific confidence. She may be nervous and uncertain of herself in many areas, but in her area, she can be a fearless conqueror. That kind of fearlessness is good and should be encouraged.

Say for instance that your daughter decides to master ice skating. Jumps and spins terrify young skaters. Until they learn some simple jumping techniques, they lack the confidence to give even simple jumps a try. In cases like this, you need to encourage her to smile in the face of fear! Laugh at it out loud if necessary! There is simply no reason even the most timid can't be encouraged in isolated instances to laugh in the face of fear and act offensively.

The problem we're trying to overcome is the belief that fear necessitates stopping. Fear does not always mean stop. In fact, sometimes it means "Charge!" harder and faster than before. Let us repeat that we don't necessarily think you should teach your girl to be fearless of everything. She should be afraid of and run from some things. But in her area of mastery, let her get the feel of overcoming fear with excitement and the confidence of victory! Winning those situations will build in her spirit a sense of excitement and confidence not available through any other means. It's the mastery identity!

Use Critic Repellent

Nobody ever built a monument to a critic. And for every girl with an idea or spark of ingenuity, there are two dozen critics. Girls who attack life always have critics, and so do masters. Encourage your girl to ignore those who riddle her ideas with criticism, caustic remarks, and derision. Young girls, especially those who seem overly sensitive to the words of others, will find criticism very difficult to ignore. Their tendency is to believe their critics without question. This is a huge error that only a wise adult can correct. Teach your girl to question the veracity of a critical opinion. Once our daughter came home from school crying. Someone had called her an idiot. I (Kathi) simply asked her, "Are you an idiot?" "No!" she huffed. "Why do you think you are not an idiot?" I continued. "Because I have a smart brain," she retorted. "Well then, they're wrong, aren't they?" I finished. She agreed. Within the framework of this matter-of-fact exchange we had established a precedent for handling future criticisms. Instead of accepting remarks at face value she could now begin to question their validity based on her knowledge of herself.

At the same time, be alert to those moments when your girl becomes the critic! Don't let an incidence go by unchecked. We have a policy that nobody is allowed to criticize unless he or she can offer a better way. This rule serves both to limit the amount of idea assassination that is rampant among kids and to encourage them to think and create on their own.

Let Her Teach You

Girls who gain mastery enjoy teaching parents and others about their subject. This is such a pronounced urge that we think it wise for you to be available, receptive, and educable when she shows up with some talent. Ask for repeated demonstrations, ask questions, ask to "see that move again," say "Go slower so I can try," and so on. Your interest has enormous unseen value to your girl.

You know how good it can feel to gain someone's interest. We recently talked to an adult woman who had to teach her mother how to drive. Our acquaintance described for us how good it felt to be able to effectively teach her mother something she had mastery over. Give your girl the opportunity to experience the thrill of sharing with you something she's mastering.

Imagination, Creativity, and Resourcefulness

There is no nation like the imagination.
Albert Einstein

Eyes that look are common; eyes that see are rare.
Unknown

Two Brainteasers

Antonio and Cleopatra were found dead in the palace. There was some broken glass and water on the floor near where their bodies lay. There was only one witness, a cat. What happened?

Using five toothpicks, build a nuclear power plant.

(Solutions appear at the end of the chapter.)

Forty Little Piggies

Some friends of ours were recently taking a long car trip. In the back seat their girls were playing quietly—suspiciously quietly. A long time had passed when suddenly appearing on the top of the front seat was a series of feet all lined up. As Mom and Dad peered over their shoulders to see what was going on, it was announced they were about to see a play performed by a troupe of feet. Dad had to watch from the rearview mirror.

The play began with standard juvenile hilarity and naturally disintegrated quickly into senseless guffaws and cheers of "Encore!" from the front seats. The girls obliged, taking off their socks and doing a smelly curtain call of a song they made up called "Forty Little Piggies Dancing in a Row" (there were four girls). It was a stinky ending to a creative car ride!

We've certainly mixed a wide range of topics so far in this book! All the topics interlock. Just like a puzzle, the more pieces you get connected the more the image begins to take shape, excitement about the effort grows, and the final product begins to come into view. That's where we find ourselves right now. The picture we're piecing together is quite beautiful. It is your girl.

In many respects, raising an extraordinary girl is an act of creation. We all begin with some raw materials. Using our own experience, wits, and convictions we focus and develop her, love her, and train her the best we know how. Then we set her free to challenge life on her own terms. It's a serious matter for those imaginative enough to see the consequences. It's a little exciting; a little scary.

You're doing great! You're a good coach. And you are about to lead your daughter into developing a trio of qualities that will serve her well throughout the rest of her life. What are they? The first quality is imagination; the second, creativity; the third, resourcefulness. Each quality leads to the next, each relies on the skill of the supporting step immediately below it, each interlocks to form a column of steps marching up toward awesome living. Winston Churchill was once paraphrased as remarking that the worst part of poverty was "never feeling anything surprising; never seeing anything beautiful; never hearing anything witty." The same elements are lacking in one's life when one has poverty of the imagination. Let's commit ourselves to making certain our daughters never experience poverty of the imagination.

Step 1: Imagination

Girls are not born creative or resourceful. They are born *imaginative*. One of our *Girls!* Team members relayed with amusement how as a child she would go into the woods with other little children in her neighborhood and "cook" lunch for everyone. She'd whip up some moss and wood chips— "veggies and meat"—and treat her little pals to some Martha Stewart hospitality! What was probably most imaginative about all this was that the little guests all ate what they were served! They probably planned to pitch in together and buy her a Foxfire cookbook for Christmas!

From forest food to paper dolls to boogie monsters, girls are imagining all sorts of things. Imagination is a raw kind of brain power. Imagination is what your brain can do if it's unconstrained. In any of the senses, our brains can create experiences and make them seem real. Imagine, if you will, taking a long whiff off the top of an ammonia bottle. You can smell it! You probably made a bad face too! Imagine taking a big, luscious bite of a tart yellow lemon. Imagine biting through slowly, tasting first the bitter rind, then the juice as it puckers your lips and runs down your cheeks. Ahhhhh! That's not fun to imagine! Your brain is quite the master of imaginary experience.

You've been able to do that kind of imagining since you were a very tiny person. Your brain can recreate more or less any experience you've ever had, and what's most interesting is it can distort and blend those memories in countless ways. The world's most powerful computers, with many millions of lines of programming code, can't do what an average three-year-old can do. Impressive!

So what do we parents do with all this native power in our girls? You have many options. Since imagination is the first step to even greater innovative talents, and since the talent is built-in, your best option is to clear the way for imagination and fuel it. Think of imagination as the engine of a car. All you need to make it run is gas. Experience is the gasoline of the mind. Focus on exposing her to sensory experiences. Let her see sunsets, look in microscopes, search through holograms. Let her hear baby birds chirp, Bach on CD, a recording of Neil Armstrong's first steps on the moon. Let her feel chicken gizzards, astonishment, high G-forces. Let her taste wild sassafras, raw fish, baker's chocolate. Let her smell perfumes in a store, dirt, and freshly copied paper. Her curiosity about the sensorial array of things is piqued in childhood, so let her gather it all in.

Do anything you can to set her imagination afire. Once we visited a national park that conducted open-air shows about the stars. One particular night an unusually colorful naturalist took us on a tour of the cosmos. He shut off all the lights in the amphitheater and simply began talking about what was "up." I'll never forget him pointing up toward the Andromeda Galaxy and saying, "That tiny patch of light is a galaxy about the size of our Milky Way. It is one of about one hundred million galaxies in the whole universe. Each one of those galaxies has over one billion stars bigger than our sun." Our kids gasped. "Over one billion stars bigger than our sun," they kept muttering. They whispered it on the walk back to our camp. They asked us about it at bedtime. They talked about it at breakfast the next morning. They kept looking up at the sun saying, "One billion stars bigger than our sun!" Three little imaginations had been irrevocably sparked.

You can have fun with your daughter doing synesthesia: the experience of combining sensory experiences. Ask her what red tastes like! Have her make the sound of softness. Ask what loudness smells like and if she can hear the sunset. She'll have great fun with these kinds of challenges, even though she may not have the slightest inkling what you mean. Imagining is one of the most natural, entertaining things young girls do. Encourage it whenever you can. Model odd forms of imagination. Ask for imaginative innovations from her. Try to outdo her at every turn!

Girls grow in their use of imagination as their brains develop. Girls become more sophisticated, pointed, and focused in their thinking, paving a new step up in innovational talent: creativity. Parents don't play much of a role in building imagination; girls are born with that. Creativity, however, is something you can influence—enormously. Let's take a look at how.

Step 2: Creativity

Creativity happens when imagination is directed, or focused, in some way. If you simply fuel a car, light up the engine, and step away, the car will careen off to wherever. That's imagination. Now, let's say someone decides to hop in and drive. That's creativity.

There is a world of opportunity in joy-riding this wild vehicle, no matter who's driving! But let's discuss these driving arrangements. Naturally, the point is to get your girl to drive herself. She will do that naturally if two conditions are met: first, if it's fun for her, and second, if she feels creativity has rewards. We've seen many girls, who have never found much fun in their own imaginations, stall their car engine before they leave the driveway. We've also seen girls who are naturally quite inventive but, for lack of support or appreciation, keep the car in the garage.

All the following suggestions for building creativity are fun. They easily pass the first requirement. Should you participate in them at home and make them a daily part of life, your daughter will find them a rewarding way to connect with you. We urge you to try them all. Remember that what we are attempting to accomplish is giving your girl the feeling of driving her own car. In our experience, it is quite difficult to predict which of these suggestions might focus her creativity. To that end, be ambitious and try many different angles.

Let's call this list our "Lambourghini List," because these suggestions are very fast and very hot! They boldly push your girl to focus her imagination into specific creative outlets. You can easily slide them into almost any family gathering, from dinner on a midsummer night to Christmas morning. They take little or no preparation and work miracles to boost family life.

- Story and parable telling
- Singing and dancing
- Winging it
- Visual and auditory arts
- Creating new words and languages
- Games and puzzles

Story and Parable Telling

Storytelling is one of the easiest creative outlets you can use. Stories can be told not only with words, but also with sound effects, mime, facial expressions, and more. You needn't be Mark Twain to tell stories. Just follow a few rules, and you'll happen on success in the most enjoyable way.

Choose a story from the news, odd relatives, tales you've heard, or weird daily events. If you want to really challenge your own creativity, make up a story from scratch. That, however, is optional. What you want is a simple story line.

Mentally or on a piece of paper, outline five story parts comprising a beginning, end, and two or three middle events. Then just simply tell them in order. It doesn't matter if it takes ten seconds or ten minutes. If you're feeling unusually bold and outrageous, add sound effects, facial expressions, or coordinated hand and body movements. Then brace yourself; you'll be an overnight sensation. Demand for your tales and antics will become constant. That's good!

As a little girl, I (Kathi) recall sitting on my bed spellbound as my dad spun one of his unforgettable "Susie and Tommy" tales. The adventures of Susie and Tommy were invented nightly in my dad's mind and recreated in ours through simple storytelling. We knew these characters' voices, faces, and personalities as if they actually existed. They had been painted in our minds by words as colorful as life. Those pictures held us in breathless, wide-eyed excitement on the edges of the bed!

In my childish mind my dad was a pro at making sounds like creaking doors, howling winds, or banging shutters. Whatever the noise, he always gave it his best try. I do know that whatever talent he may have lacked we made up for with wild imagination and anticipation! He could have been the worst storyteller in the world and we wouldn't have ever known. To us, he was the storymaster, and we hung perilously on every breath! We couldn't get enough of those adventurous capers and good morals.

Do your girl a favor and tell her a simple story. Do your best. She'll fill in the bad spots and remember you as the greatest storyteller that ever lived.

Parables are a natural extension of storytelling. They are brief stories told for the purpose of imparting wisdom. In the ancient tradition, parables contain great wisdom. It shouldn't surprise us that the greatest parable teller of all time was Jesus. Take note that most of Jesus' parables didn't actually happen, but the truth or wisdom in them was so profound it didn't matter. They could easily have happened, and all those who heard them knew it.

Don't worry about your parables not being true. Just make certain that the wisdom is clear and the lessons firm. We would suggest that the best way to do this is by establishing for yourself a list of "life lessons" you want your girl to learn. These could be sayings such as "Honesty is the best policy," "Chastity brings greater happiness than imprudence," "Save money, for a rainy day will come," and so on. Make the list rather brief, perhaps five or six lessons you think are the most profound. Then, spend some time (weeks or months if necessary) searching for wise tales that illustrate those life lessons you've decided are important. You can find these tales in your own real-life experiences, old fables, biographies, and library anthologies. Write those tales down someplace where they will not be lost and tell them to your girl at opportune moments over the next year.

The teaching power of parables is potent, especially if you can find clever stories that serve as variations on each of your themes. Keep your parables handy; you will use them.

Telling parables is a great tool for your daughter to learn to use. Simply teach her by showing her how you do it. Explain that you'll be searching for the meaning in her stories. This in effect gives her permission and encouragement to speak to you in an entirely creative way.

It's interesting, that as girls get a bit older, they're actually quite good at intentionally imbedding requests, problems, suggestions, and complaints inside a story.

Singing and Dancing

Singing and dancing are excellent means by which girls can express imagination. They can dramatically enhance and add novelty to verbal forms of communication. Singing gives your girl the words to use, and dancing gives her a wordless form in which to express herself. There isn't much for you to do; simply turn on the music and usually girls will listen and move. It's impossible for most of us, especially young kids, to stay still when we hear certain types of music.

It's lots of fun to create songs and dances. Encourage your daughter to slip out of the mold of singing like the singers on tapes or dancing like the people around her. Press this point by encouraging her to make up her own songs and tunes, experiment with new rhythms, add innovative lyrics to old tunes, move in unexpected ways, and then combine these elements in fun, fresh ways!

Now let us warn you: This may be difficult to take. The songs may be horrid and the dances pathetic. Be patient and attentive! Encourage her every squeak and move. Remember, *fun* and *rewarding*!

Winging It

"Winging it" is doing clowny things with everyday items. Girls are natural-born wingers. Girls love to take broomsticks or mops and dance arm-in-handle with them. They use pots and pans as drums and cymbals. They use forks for microphones. The list of wingable objects is endless, and your daughter's imagination drives very smoothly on this wing-it road.

We like to actively encourage this sort of nonsense. It works the best if you lead the way by improvising with various objects yourself. One time the kids and I (Kathi) were driving down the road, and one of the kids found a Magic Marker under the seat. There was trumpet music playing on the car radio, so of course they all began taking turns blowing the marker like a trumpet. They threw it up to me and asked me to toot it, but I refused. Instead, while stopped at a red light, I took the lid off and wrote on the driver's side window, "I'm tired of you kids blowing in my ear! Signed, Mr. Marker."

The kids were stunned, not by the message, but by the fact that I'd write on the car window! After they collected themselves, they read the note and smirked. What would you guess happened then? You're right; they all wanted the marker so they could write replies on their windows! By the end of that ride, "Mr. Marker" had a personality all his own and had written his opinions all over the car windows.

Encourage your daughter to be inventive with ordinary objects. It can be loads of fun. But more than that, it teaches her to see the world in lots of different ways. Creative people know how to manipulate their same old world in new and fresh ways.

Visual and Auditory Arts

Your daughter may not be a Picasso or Pavarotti, but you need to outfit your home as if she were! Every home should have things that draw—pencils, paints, computers. Every home should have things that make noise—pots and pans, whistles, Steinways. Items like old clothes for dress up, puppets, chalk, used greeting cards, stickers, boxes, buttons, and old jewelry can be kept in a special cabinet or drawer, your "creativity booster" center. We've found it very useful to have one spot where kids can find all sorts of tools with which to be creative in different visual and auditory ways.

Keep the supplies very simple and inexpensive. The free things are the most fun! For visual arts, help your girl trace funny pictures, make collages from newspaper pictures, cut out paper dolls, make mud animals. An absolute requirement is to display your daughter's creations for the world to see. On the auditory side, create a pot-and-pan band, fill glasses to different depths with water to make different tones when tapped, play a song by opening your mouth and tapping the top of your head with sticks.

Your girl should learn early that creative expression is normal and fun. It is a chance for girls to give something of themselves to a world needing to hear from them. You really cannot stifle the human imagination from somehow expressing itself. The history of mankind and a basic familiarity with the nature of people prove that people must express their imaginations creatively. In essence, your daughter will find ways to express her imagination in creative ways regardless of what you do. Be that as it may, try to provide obvious places for imagination to flow out.

The key drawback of many of today's toys is that they require so little creativity. Most of these toys don't use a child's creativity. They simply entertain the imagination. On the other hand, any form of art is the natural, focused expression of imagination. It gives back to the world by inspiring others, something playing with toys cannot do. But art is work; it takes effort. Don't let your girl get creatively flabby! Hand her a brush and a landscape!

Creating New Words and Languages

In my work with elementary school children, I (Kathi) often discovered siblings who had developed their own language. Though complicated systems of language are very rarely created, unique phrases among siblings are actually common. If you have siblings, to this day you probably have little words, sounds, or phrases holding special meaning to all of you. Perhaps you still use them when talking to one another, and most likely you still laugh! Intentionally creating words and private expressions with your child is inventive.

We've tried this in the past with kids as a means to build rapport, maintain privacy, and talk about something that perhaps there is no word for. One time I (Bill) worked with a family of small, quiet children. They had a strict father who prided himself on being "no nonsense" and was always quick to lecture me about his forward-thinking parenting techniques. He was a real whiz all right: His kids thought he was Hitler. Everybody thought it, but they couldn't say it. As counselees, it's important to speak about troubles, but the children were adamant about not mentioning anything negative about their dad.

So we created our own unique language. I suggested, for instance, that whenever they wanted to say their dad was being a grump, we'd say he was being a *woober*. "Yep, Dad's a little *woober* today!" This busted the kids up every time and allowed us to talk about a topic that was fearful and threatening to them all. What was most interesting is that these children began to make up words for all kinds of things: sadness, being excited about school being over, feeling strange about wearing ugly clothes, etc. I'm certain that anybody listening in on our conversations would have thought us a bunch of salad heads, but it was creative and very effective.

Introduce to your girl secret codes, sign language, sounds, and odd phrases to which you assign specific meaning. For example, raise your eyebrow or wink to mean "Pass the salt" at dinner, spell out "I love you" using your fingers as letters, clear your throat to mean "Look to the right." Once you show them this new realm of expression, you'll all have a lot of creative fun!

Games and Puzzles

It bears repeating that many of the toys kids play with today stir their imagination, but not their creativity. (Keep the difference clearly in mind: Imagination is the natural energy, and creativity is the focus.) Games and puzzles, however, make girls *do* something with their imagination. You needn't go out and spend a wad to retool your game selection. You can just as easily make up games and puzzles or borrow them from a library.

If you are going to make them up, we have some suggestions. First, go outside if you can. Don't try to teach creativity and originality cloistered in some stuffy house. Go outdoors, where imagination is liberated! Second, make your games and puzzles physically active. Creativity, unlike imagination, needs to be expressed *outwardly*. Physical action is always the preferred mode of expression in girls. Last, remember that it's better to do many small puzzles and games than one long one. Keep your creativity time brief and encourage her to participate. Keep the action moving. Then she will look forward to more!

You can make up all sorts of simple games and puzzles within these bounds. Get on bikes and follow a bird to see where it goes, play hide-and-seek, sit under a tree and play twenty questions, try a magic trick, create a new way to play hopscotch, hold an impromptu scavenger hunt! Unravel nature's mysteries, such as identifying footprints, bird nests, and fallen leaves. These activities can really be fun and, though simple, can ignite an enormous spark of creativity in your girl!

Step 3: Resourcefulness

In reviewing our information for this chapter, it occurred to us that the next step lying directly above creativity is doing something specific with your creative talent, in other words, using your creative talent to help you in some way. Since most of us don't use our creativity to make a living, do we have a daily need for innovation besides entertainment? Can creativity help us out day to day? You bet! We can use it for solving problems. Creativity helps us discover ways to fix things that sidetrack us or cause difficulty.

Building the resourcefulness step in your girl is, in our opinion, one of the most important things you can possibly do. That's because most girls don't become resourceful without some direction.

Simple problem solving comes more or less naturally to healthy girls. What does not come so easily is a sense of comfort in handling or solving difficult problems. One of the greatest by-products of turning creativity into resourcefulness is that your daughter can experience an enormous reduction in anxiety when faced with life's problems. *Finding or creating solutions* can and should become second nature to your girl. Build it a step at a time.

Teach her first to *relax and slow down* when a challenge first appears. Far too many girls wilt in panic when faced with troubles. That response comes from either modeling parents' panic or from a lack of self-confidence to think on their feet and resourcefully find answers. It's common for girls in this situation to become erratic and flustered, further adding to their sense of internal chaos. Girls left stewing in situations like this learn only to wait for others to fix their problems. Not good.

That sense of panic needs to be extricated over time by patiently demonstrating that problems are slowly solved one simple step at a time. Tell your daughter to take a deep breath and remain in control; she may even need to sit down and "chill out" for a while. She can actually solve almost any trouble with nothing more than a strong ability to keep her head!

The next step in resourcefulness training is teaching your daughter that problems and difficulties *always have more than one solution*. This fact comes as a revelation to many girls. Girls watch us handle difficulties day to day and are accustomed to our being decisive in what appear to be simple questions. We adults know, however, that life rarely hurls us simple problems, and oftentimes we must be satisfied to simply do the best we can in bad circumstances. Our girls may never see the conflicts, trade-offs, and compromises we must handle to make life move on. We make it all look easy.

The best way to teach your girl that all problems have many solutions is in a real situation. Within a relaxed conversation ask her to help you solve some simple problem you are faced with today. Explain the problem as simply as possible, then ask her to help you create a list of solutions. Three or four will be fine! Whatever the problem is she'll most likely stall at two, perhaps three, ideas. This is when it gets fun.

Recall in chapter 6 that we discussed the nature of straight-line, step-by-step logic. We suggested that this sort of logic was the building block of common sense. We also suggested at that time that there was another type of logic referred to as "lateral" logic, which played a role in creativity and problem solving. Lateral logic invokes one's creativity to help make difficult jumps in logic. The story of Antonio and Cleopatra and the toothpick challenge at the beginning of this chapter are classic problems requiring lateral logic. You can be commonsensical all day and not come close to solving those mysteries.

Some problems require you to break out of your old mold of thinking and think in new ways. Let's say for instance you were trying to invent several new solutions to the problem of getting the dishes rinsed and loaded into the dishwasher every night. Some direct, logical solutions might include your becoming a better time manager, getting help from some of the kids, or having the kids rent you a maid. Lateral logic would suggest radically different solutions: eating right out of the pans, using paper plates, going to McDonalds, T.V. dinners, or Hark!—everybody doing their own dishes!

Lateral logic encourages boldness and originality. (The kids cleaning up after themselves certainly would be original!) Encourage your girl to practice wild lateral logic. It's fun and rewarding! Collect a long list of those lateral thoughts. Don't stop simply at the ones that seem correct or obvious, but press on to try to come up with weirder solutions. Sometimes they are the best! Girls find this exercise fun and freeing. Can you see how problem solving under these conditions suddenly becomes fun? Fixing problems is a joy, for it's free license to think up wild and crazy solutions!

Encourage your girl to seek the input of others. If she learns the truth of the old saying that "two heads are better than one," she'll be loaded with resourcefulness. In our family we habitually encourage the kids to ask one another for problem-solving ideas. External input might in fact be one of the finest sources of lateral logic around. As long as your daughter recognizes that the sources of solutions can be found beyond herself, she'll use them.

Getting outside input is even better if she can find an expert in the problem she's trying to fix. Talk about great lateral logic! I (Bill) once worked with a girl who was very boyish looking. It bothered her greatly. She was about eleven years old with scraggly hair, slim hips, and a rather muscular build. She knew she stood out. I confessed to her that making girls look feminine was not my strong suit, but I encouraged her to consider that there are people in the world who are experts in that. Nobody had ever suggested that to her! "Oh yeah," I said, "they're all over. Most of them work in the mall." I had no idea what I was talking about, but I guessed that somebody someplace had some ideas about what could be done. Guess where my little counselee wanted to go right after our session?

I encouraged her to arrange a trip to a beauty salon and ask for the person who is best at making girls look like beautiful women. She wasn't sure what to do but thought she could place some phone calls to find the right store, ask her mom for a ride, and maybe look at some magazines to find a look that suited her. Then, lo and behold, one day she came to our appointment with her hair fixed up! All by herself, she'd arranged the proper circumstances and found herself an expert. She was very proud of herself, as she should have been.

The girl was resourceful. Every problem has several solutions if your girl just knows where to look. Teach her to look once, look twice, and then keep on looking until she finds the answer that suits her.

* * *

The solutions to the opening riddles are simple. First, Antonio and Cleopatra are goldfish; the cat knocked them off their stand onto the floor and broke their bowl, killing them.

The five toothpicks? Well, after a lot of thought I think your only option is to find the head of the Atomic Energy Commission, jump him in an alley, and hold him hostage with the toothpicks until he agrees to build the plant! Short of that, go out to dinner and use the toothpicks after the meal to sit, pick, and ponder some more. There have to be more solutions!

Decisions, Decisions!

I (Bill) can still hear my dad saying, "Use your head and make good decisions out there." He'd always say that as I was leaving for a night on the town or a friend's house for dinner. He knew me pretty well and was cagey about making those father-knows-best remarks. You see, I was sort of a Goofus and Gallant type kid (you remember, those two characters from *Highlights* magazine; one was rude and obnoxious, and the other was kind and courteous). At home I was Gallant: I'd always shut off lights when I left the room, pass the serving tray to the left at dinner, and use the correct fork. Away from home, though, I was Goofus: I'd make rude noises, blow my nose on the tablecloth, and eat my food without chewing. My dad was no dummy. He was probably that way as a boy, too.

Getting your girl to the point of deliberately using her own good reckoning and making good decisions on her own is what this chapter is all about. As we discovered in chapter 6, common sense has structure. We've seen, however, that possessing good sense and using it are quite different. We all know many stories of those who, though knowing better, did something really dumb and paid an enormously high price

That kind of situation can happen to even well-meaning girls. There is no fail-safe way to protect your girl from wandering into messes like those. You can, however, build in her the habit of making good, thoughtful decisions.

Our girls grow up and leave us all too soon. They leave to do the best they can in a world known to eat people. All they have for navigation is what you've taught them and their own good sense, which hopefully they'll use! Jo had the following conversation with Mr. March in *Little Men*:

> [Jo] "I only want to give these children a home in which they can be taught the few simple things which will help to make life less hard to them when they go out to fight their battles in the world. Honesty, courage, industry, faith in God, their fellow creatures, and themselves; that is all I try for."
>
> [Mr. March] "That is everything. Give them these helps, then let them go to work out their life as men and women; and whatever their success or failure is, I think they will remember and bless your efforts."[11]

Let this be your battle cry. Your daughter will remember you and some time in the future bless you for the efforts you made to teach her.

We all know our girls quite well and must admit they probably have a little Jekyll and Hyde in them. They change when they are not in our presence. This is no crime; kids are kids, and we expect it. What can we give our girls that transcends their personality alteration? Can we implant in them anything that will remain steadfast even during those inevitable moments when life turns crazy?

This summer we went to a nationally renowned amusement park. In its repertoire of nauseation machines is one of the fiercest roller coasters in the world. I (Bill) was standing in line behind a group of bold and happy preteen girls. Among them was a girl who was wearing a T-shirt endorsing "No Fear." It seemed to be their theme this day, because as we waited in line they kept firing one another up with variations of "No Fear! Yeh, NO FEAR!" I'm not the smartest guy in town, but I sensed some fear.

Then we got into the coaster. They all got quiet, and when they did venture a phrase, it was croaked. The loud bragging turned into meekness. Meekness disintegrated into hopeless laments as this vile contraption began to move. Their faces went pale, and the laments gave way to one of the girls *crying*. One of the more cocksure (the one with the shirt) began to ridicule her weeping comrade. *Nice friends,* I thought. I suddenly heard my dad saying, "Make good decisions," and I realized this little bawl baby should have known my dad. Too late; we were at the top of the hill, and this little band of fearnots was about to be introduced to a new dimension of terror.

I don't really remember what happened after that because the G-forces of the ride got me spacey. But you should've seen Ms. Tearful at the conclusion of the tour. She was a mess. Sobbing without taking much more than a breath between sobs. I guess sometimes fear isn't a bad idea. Nice, well-intentioned girls can get in over their heads quickly.

Start Early

The efficient way to implant good decision-making habits is to start as early as possible. We heard some sage once say that either "we build habits or the habits build us." That's a guru-like way of saying habits are going to be in place in your life anyway, so you might just as well do what you can to choose them. Decision-making habits are the most reliable and manageable when deliberately chosen.

How early do you start? As close to the beginning as possible. We see every reason to encourage your girl from the start to make good decisions. Does that mean you should let her make all her own decisions? Absolutely not! *Kids should not be allowed to make serious decisions without strong parental guidance.* Should a two-year-old decide what she'll eat for dinner? No! Should a five-year-old decide where she wants to go to school? No! Should a seven-year-old decide what she'll watch on television? No! Should a ten-year-old decide whether or not she is going to go to church? No!

If we were reading this chapter before a live audience, half would be cheering and the other half would be booing. The cheerleaders would be delighted someone was suggesting they take control of their kids. The boo-bearers would be upset that their kids would never get the chance to learn any executive skills in such a stifling atmosphere. Both opinions have their points. The challenge in balancing these perspectives amounts to risk versus overprotection. Too much risk, and your girl careens through life without having learned solid skills upon which to think and act. Too much overprotection, and your girl lacks street sense about how to deal with complicated, difficult, and often confusing real-life situations.

Let's offer some guidelines. There is a way to get to the solid middle ground. Bring your daughter along in her decision making at a deliberate, step-by-step pace. The steps of decision making for girls should look something like this: Define what decision needs to be made; examine options; and choose. You can count on girls to learn this progression backwards; first they want the fun part, making the choice! That's why letting your daughter make her own decisions about too many things too early builds disastrous habits. She can easily begin to think decision making is no big deal.

Redefinition

Let's start with defining the problem. As we said, from a girl's perspective the only important part of decision making is the choices themselves. We as adults know that the choices in a decision depend on how we first conceive of the problem. Your girl needs to discover this fact for herself. Start by taking some time to probe her with questions about the problem she is trying to solve rather than the choices she's dreamt up.

You may, for instance, be asked to help her decide what to buy a friend for a birthday. From her perspective, all she sees in her mind is aisle after aisle of choices (toys). If you ask her to define her problem, she'll likely say it's "to decide which toy to buy." Just for fun (and instruction), let's say you suggest she define the problem differently. Suggest that her problem is really to figure out some way to *surprise* her friend. That definition of the problem opens up all kinds of fun options, such as buying her a kitten, making a piñata, getting an autographed picture of her favorite star, or writing her a poem!

This is where resourcefulness comes in. You can redefine the problem dozens of times every day in either real or made-up situations. Your daughter is facing problems all the time. Her problems range between how she's going to do her hair to what she's going to wear to what to do after school to what to read or watch on television. These simple decisions all involve solving specific problems, problems that can be defined and redefined many different ways.

More Options

The redefinition exercise opens up all kinds of new options. But girls still make fast-impulse decisions based on only the most obvious choices, no matter how wide the list of options. It is a rare girl who can scan the options and say, "Gee, I think I need to create some *better* options for myself!" Just the opposite usually happens. Since decision making can be confusing, girls simply want the fewest possible options with the most direct path of deciding. That system works well in deciding what shoes to wear, but not in solving the bigger problems they'll face.

Teach your daughter to say to herself, *There are always more options.* Here is resourcefulness again. We encourage the girls we know to think wildly about other options. I (Kathi) routinely teach this concept to my students at school.

After presenting a specific situation and having them identify the problem, I encourage them to generate two or three
possible solutions. They can generally offer two options without help. Then I dream up ridiculous options to spark their
creativity. With encouragement they soon offer more. This
process of finding options is usually simple for adults but
must be demonstrated for and encouraged in young people.
I practice this skill over and over throughout the school year
until my students can readily list five or more options for each
situation I present. I feel confident that with this skill intact
they will be able to successfully attack any problem that arises.

Teach your daughter a certain voraciousness about making her list of options as large as possible. Encourage her to
seek the input of others. Teach her that when she reaches the
dead end of her own imagination, others (like you) are just
getting warmed up! Her list of resources to build more
options includes you, siblings, friends, teachers, librarians,
encyclopedias, and others.

Choosing an Option

We've seen that the wider the range of options, the better
opportunity your girl has to make a good decision. The
process of actually making the choice among the options
depends to a great deal on the age of your girl. As we've mentioned, young girls should not be making major decisions.
It is quite healthy, however, for them to start getting used to
scanning their options and picking. The rule of thumb we
encourage is letting your girl make simple, well contained
decisions inside all areas of her life.

Should she decide what she's going to eat at the age of
three? No. But she can decide among a group of options.
She can, for instance, eat two spoonfuls of peas or two spoonfuls of spinach. It's her choice, but you must help focus the
range of choices: "You must eat a green vegetable." She won't
always like her options, but childhood can be tough at times.

As you do these option-building exercises, she'll grow more successful in suggesting alternatives to those you have provided for her. It's been our experience that the best thing to do as she ages and becomes more sophisticated in her suggestions is to seriously consider her alternative on one condition: that she explain to you why her suggestion is better than yours and can demonstrate how her best interests will be served by taking that option. We've been repeatedly stunned by the depth of insight and thought kids can generate when faced with this sort of challenge.

The first demand is straightforward. She will easily be able to give you endless reasons why her option is better than yours. What may not be so easy is explaining how her interests are better served by her idea than yours. We have a solution to that, but it requires introducing her to TimeFraming and giving her an ability to show you where she thinks her decisions will lead her.

TimeFraming

I (Bill) developed TimeFraming as a new way to communicate with kids. TimeFraming is built on the simple premise that kids are visually oriented, thus handicapped in the world of words. We as adults rely heavily on words, especially for communication. Therein lies an obvious and unavoidable dilemma between parent and child. How are we to bridge the gap? Kids want to communicate with their parents, and vice versa. But the gulf created by words seems impassable. It is passable.

TimeFraming capitalizes on a universal human ability to perceive life better with pictures than with words. It puts the flow of life into pictures. It works by drawing pictures of life events inside a series of boxes, or "frames," connected by arrows that show the flow of action through time. A simple TimeFraming sequence of a real-life problem might look like this:

I originally used TimeFraming to unravel the sequences that led up to and followed problem situations my own children were having. Rather than saying, "Oh my dear little sweety poopsy, tell me what happened to you in this horrid situation!" I would say, "Tell me how this whole thing started." I would then draw a picture of what they described.

Let me illustrate this. My daughter, Jessie, was having a spat with a close friend. She was miserable, and my attempts to get her talking were futile. I sat next to her on the couch with a legal pad and bright red flair-tip marker in my hand. She loves those markers, and I knew it. She was trying to read a magazine but she was crying.

I drew a large box in the middle of the page and, handing her the pen, asked her to draw a picture of what happened between her and her pal. She quickly grabbed the pen and began sketching.

When she had finished I tore off that page and put it on the floor, then handed the pad back and simply asked, "What happened after this?" She again began drawing furiously. Her picture was of her running home crying. I tore off that picture and placed it on the floor to the right of the original. I mentioned to her that one led to the next. I handed the pad back to her and said simply, "What happened then?" She drew a picture of us sitting on the couch drawing pictures. I then took the marker and added some humorous details to the picture, which made her giggle. I drew a smiley face on her face in the picture, tore it off, and placed it on the floor.

I then had two options: One, I could ask her to draw pictures of what happened prior to the blow-out with her friend—the sequence of events leading up to the problem. Then I would lay them out side by side to show how the problem unfolded. Second, I could have her draw pictures of what she thought she ought to do in the immediate future. Either way, you can see that we would quickly develop a long line of frames spread out on the floor describing events as they unfolded over time: TimeFrames.

We chose the latter. I suggested that she draw out what she was going to do next. She had no ideas. I grabbed the pen and drew a picture of her eating a sandwich. She grabbed it back from me and drew a picture of her playing with the dog. I retrieved the pen from her and drew a picture of her doing homework with a smile on her face. We laid all these pictures out in a row on the floor. This entire interaction, taking about fifteen minutes, was conducted with almost no talking at all.

We left the picture trail on the floor all night. She ended up her evening living out the frames exactly as we'd proposed them in the afternoon! She played with the dog and finished her homework. Pictures are powerful to girls.

This approach is peerless in its power to communicate clearly and rapidly. It is an excellent system for working with children about their problems. Beyond pointing out how common troubles unfold, it's a fabulous tool to use to suggest courses of action in the wake of some event, to explore options and where those options might lead, and to explore how particular options serve the person's best interests.

TimeFraming is in short a decision-making tool, an "options exploration" tool. Use it in having your daughter explain how her interests are better served by her ideas than yours. Draw a frame of her at the present. To the right of that, draw a frame listing the new options she's suggesting. Then (this might take a few minutes, but they'll be very well spent), draw numerous lines emanating from the frame on the right, going off in several directions, as many arrows as there are options to explore. Next, you will want to draw a series of frames depicting to the best of your ability what you and your daughter think will happen.

You as an experienced adult can look at each of the options she's suggesting and predict what the outcome of it will be at least two or three frames ahead without drawing them. Your daughter cannot do that! That's why kids often make dumb decisions! Using TimeFraming, however, she will be able to begin peering ahead in some orderly manner, and what she will see there might even surprise her! Just take each option and, by drawing, demonstrate the inevitable consequences of choosing it. It's eye-opening.

Use TimeFraming in any combination or creative way you like. The power of drawing what otherwise would require words will amaze you. Icons are the words of childhood. Once your daughter is well versed in drawing out where her life is going, you'll be better able to see what she's thinking. Best of all, though, she'll have a method of clearly looking ahead to see how her choices affect her interests.

Practice Makes Perfect

Experience has taught us that practicing these simple steps of decision making (defining what decision needs to be made, developing options, and choosing which will serve her best in the long run) daily in real-life settings puts girls at ease with the whole decision-making process. There's no substitute for reality. The more decisions your daughter makes, and the more feedback you provide, the more quickly she'll become skilled.

Feedback. Hmmm. Most girls don't dig feedback, especially from you. You'll find (if you haven't already) that girls don't like to be reminded of their mistakes. The less of a big deal you make of her mistakes and miscalculations—the more matter-of-fact you can be—the less the lesson stings. We're dealing with girls whose minds have much development to undergo. We want to stretch them slightly, certainly not to the point where they get shredded by frustration, but to the point where they feel challenged yet confident in decision making. To that end, let's look at six major mistakes parents make in teaching girls to make decisions.

1. Not allowing girls to make any errors
2. Saying "I told you so"
3. Letting emotions get in the way
4. Ignoring the power of her role models and heroes
5. Allowing procrastination
6. Falling for the "I don't know" and "I don't care" excuses

Mistake #1: Not Allowing Girls to Make Any Errors

How do you expect girls to learn if they don't stumble and bumble once in a while? Now when they are very young, as we've discussed, narrow their choices for them, but narrow them just enough so that some of their choices may actually end up being uncomfortable. You've heard stories of parents who let their children eat pure chocolate for dinner "just to teach them a lesson." We don't condone that choice, but the idea of letting our kids make choices that we know will be hard on them isn't such a bad idea, no matter what their age. Girls learn fast when we let them learn from their mistakes. Mistakes can be your best friend.

Not long ago our family had an experience that illustrates this fact. The kids were doing the normal juvenile thing of saying that they could do a better job shopping and cooking than we. That wasn't a good thing for them to brag about. We challenged them: We'd figure out what we spent weekly for food as a family, then figure out how much we spent per person. We agreed to give them that money to spend on themselves for food for the whole week. There was only one rule: If they ran out of food before the end of the week, tough luck. They happily agreed!

They planned well. We were really proud of them. They bought food we would not have bought, but they seemed pleased with their choices. There were lots of T.V. dinners, frozen "seafood" (frozen fish-like meat matter), and ice cream bars. We can still remember their thrill coming home from the store, hungry and ready to eat their favorite item. Their excitement slowly eroded as they realized that all the goodies they bought didn't taste as good as the pictures on the boxes looked, and nowhere near as good as Mom's cooking. It was a less than tasty experience.

By mid-week, they had a new perspective on our normal (read *boring*) cuisine. Though they had enough food to last through the week, they were beginning to hint that they'd be glad when the experiment was over. We just kept ooohing and aaaahing about their finely packaged imitation food. "Too bad you can't eat the box; come to think of it the box probably wouldn't have tasted much worse."

But these are things we all must learn. Don't stand in the way of your girl's education. Always remind her that results of decisions are largely predictable, and if she uses your help, she can see many things in the future she might not have known she could see.

Mistake #2: Saying "I Told You So"

The "I told you so's" are something you must avoid. It's just so great to be right, but you're not winning anything by rubbing your girl's nose in your brilliance. Rather, take the time to give easy, harmless feedback. Simply point things out. "Is that what you wanted to have happen?" is always a good way to start, especially when some decision she made ended in disaster. Such questions asked innocently produce little or no defensiveness. In most cases they'll get her talking about the outcomes of decisions she's made and what she thinks of them.

Many parents think it's their responsibility to give feed-back. Parental "feedback," however, is seldom heard by our girls. That's because we preach too much. Girls shut their ears when they hear our preaching. Rather, ask your daughter first if she's interested in your comments or observations. If she says yes, be sure to get her to agree that she will listen completely, and carefully consider what you say. There's no sense in throwing pearls before swine. If she says no, simply suggest that you've got ideas and you aren't going anywhere. In the event that she develops an interest in what you have to offer, you'll share it with her.

When she gives you permission to speak, make your points sharp and simple. Long, drawn out sermonettes will be ignored. Speak directly and to the point, and if she interrupts with some excuse or comment, remind her of her commit-ment to hear you out. It's only fair. Try to engage her in a simple conversation about her decision.

As always, ask lots of questions. Questioning is by far the superior way to analyze decisions and discover new and bet-ter ways to make future decisions. It's a very powerful approach.

Mistake #3: Letting Emotions Get in the Way

All girls allow emotions to sway decisions. Most adults do it, too! This reality is part of the reason we don't allow our kids to make many decisions! All we would recommend here is remembering that though you cannot stop the influence of emotions on decision making, you can point it out. Unfor-tunately, the emotions inside decisions are not clearly seen at the time of the choice. They can only be clearly recognized in hindsight. But as we earlier demonstrated, girls don't have much fore- or hindsight. We need to be their eyes.

In most cases, your daughter will never see the effects of emotions in her decisions. Happiness, anger, sadness, the "blues"—all these can play enormous roles in determining the decisions she makes. Be quick to ask how decisions might change if her mood were better: "Would you choose this if you were in a better mood?" Questions of this manner open her mind to possibilities she cannot see but can certainly understand. You do her a great favor by pointing her in these directions.

Mistake #4: Ignoring the Power of Her Role Models and Heroes

Role models have a great influence on a girl's life. Girls have an affinity to these people, whether they are real people or fictional characters. We think it's good to capitalize on this influence. If for example her hero is Lois Lane of *Superman* fame, ask her what kind of decision Lois might make on this or that subject. You will be amazed that though your little girl may be confused by a decision, she can quickly and easily imagine what her hero might do and come up with very wise and flexible alternatives.

Certainly the strength and propriety of these options depend totally on her models and heroes, but prompt her anyway and listen to what she creates. You might also ask her to imagine what *you* might do in any one of various circumstances. Wouldn't that be intriguing! You may well discover some erroneous impressions she has about you, what you believe, and the decisions you would make. Merely prompt her with the suggestions, and prepare thyself.

Do not underestimate the power that exists now inside the head of your girl to create great options and make good choices based on her models.

Mistake #5: Allowing Procrastination

Girls procrastinate for many reasons. Sometimes waiting is a very good idea. The problem with waiting is that it can become procrastination and procrastination can become a habit. Encourage your daughter not to dawdle on decisions, but to make them promptly. Dawdling creates anxiety and frustration for a girl, so encourage her to make a choice and move on. Following the suggestions made in earlier chapters, if you encourage a sense of fearlessness and a sense that she cannot make many mistakes that cannot be fixed, you will be encouraging decisiveness and boldness. Those qualities will serve her well into adulthood.

Mistake #6: Falling for the "I Don't Know" and "I Don't Care" Excuses

What can we say? These phrases seem to be some girls' best friends, especially as these girls approach adolescence. Let's cut to the core: *First, girls do know how they feel about things* and *second, girls do care.* It just takes some insistence to get them to 'fess up to what they feel inside.

Regardless of age, make it a point to press your daughter to speak about what she knows and cares about. Don't let her *ever* weasel out of a decision by copping one of these excuses! It sets a bad precedent. We recommend that you get in her face immediately if she starts to resort to this style of thinking. Stop the habit.

A Big Decision

Making good decisions is basic to a happy, productive life. For better or worse you cannot always be around when your daughter makes most of her choices. How she makes her choices when you are not present depends entirely on what kind of value base she possesses. Any flaw or inconsistency in that base will be magnified in the decisions she makes.

You must take great care to contribute to this base in the most effective way possible. What you do in this regard is more important than any other opportunity you now have. What's a substantial and reliable base on which to build? That is a very good question, and the right answer will help your girl develop into an extraordinary woman.

Created to Last

> If you don't stand for something, you'll fall for anything.
>
> *Anonymous*

> Let the little children come to me, and do not hinder them, for the kingdom of God belongs to such as these.
>
> *Mark 10:14*

> I tell you the truth, if you have faith as small as a mustard seed, you can say to this mountain, "Move from here to there" and it will move.
>
> *Matthew 17:20–21*

Exuberance

Did you happen to notice how excited we are about girls? We're frequently asked in our seminars how we can be so excited about girls and about the future when things seem so unsure and frightening. Haven't we reason to tremble and quake at the prospects of what the world is becoming? Why do we smile so much? We usually respond by noting that we have a foundation of enormous faith fortifying a tall column of optimism. It's not a blind faith but a highly specific commitment that creates in us reasons to feel both secure and satisfied. Most people are interested in knowing more about that.

We've spent the bulk of this book talking about building the qualities of a winning girl. We've spoken about building her heart, her mental skills, her physical talents, her innovative abilities. You're building a girl who's bound to be extraordinary. But you know, if she can speak with the king's English but has no love, her voice is just a creaking annoyance. If she's smart enough to reveal mysteries never before known or has the power to move mountains but doesn't have any love in her, she's powerless. If she gives all she has to the poor or lets herself be burned at the stake for her cause but can't love, she's a vacuum. If she can do everything in this book to within a hair of perfection but has not love, she's simply empty.

Consider that:

> Love never gives up.
> Love cares for others more than for self.
> Love doesn't want what it doesn't have.
> Love doesn't strut,
> Doesn't have a swelled head,
> Doesn't force itself on others,
> Isn't always "me first,"
> Doesn't fly off the handle,
> Doesn't keep score of the sins of others,
> Doesn't revel when others grovel,
> Takes pleasure in the flowering of truth,
> Puts up with anything,
> Trusts God always,
> Always looks for the best,
> Never looks back,
> But keeps going to the end.

Eugene H. Peterson
The Message[12]

Now that's winning! Where in the world can you get some love like that? You can't get it out of a book or tape series. You can't generate it yourself and plug it into your daughter like software. Love like this needs to come from a source larger than us. The route to it requires an act of radical faith.

Radical Faith

One of the hardest things to "sell" to the American public is that faith is something they need. Ninety-nine percent of Americans think God is wonderful but optional. Many reading this book believe that their faith (however it's defined) is sufficiently strong and proper for the times we face. There are many varieties of religious belief from which to choose, and chances are high that you've adopted one. These can include Christianity, Islam, scientology, Buddhism, unitarianism, Hinduism, atheism, agnosticism, and others. We hope you're satisfied with your choice.

Anyone who promotes the idea that true happiness and lifelong steadfastness *requires* faith spits into a cold headwind. Nobody wants to hear that, but it's true! We'd rather buy our happiness and steadfastness than find it through some sort of commitment to faith. The faith we prefer is really more of a convenience than a way of life. It's not really alive but more like a moosehead trophy we hang on the wall. This sort of faith, though common, lacks spontaneity and power; it's stuffed and dusty, an old showpiece with little value other than as a conversation piece.

Unfortunately, faith—the real kind that leads to an extraordinary life—must be active and sharable. It must be capable of growth and have a long history of lasting over difficult periods of time. It must be capable of survival in a harsh environment and be a beacon when the rest of our world falls to pieces. In short, our faith must be alive.

Not too many religions are really alive. In fact we've found that all the world's great religions revolve around ideas rather than around people. These great religions of the world have had proponents who wisely and forcefully articulated ways of life to follow that are beyond us, to which we need to stretch and conform ourselves. Nobody can actually be said to have achieved the goals of those faiths, for the goals are by definition unattainable. They always require just a little more meditation, prayer, commitment, caring, or worship. These religions always stay just a little bit out of reach. Except for one.

Allow Us to Make a Bold Suggestion

Life is a serious matter, and a lightweight faith is pointless. There is one great world religious faith of power and gravity vastly superior to the others. Let us be bold and suggest you attach yourself to God's greatest gift, Jesus, and help your girl become attached to him too. We're not referring to a garden-variety Christianity.

Girls, you will recall, are experiential beings. They understand relationships with people and seek to enmesh themselves within them. No other organized world religion allows the believer to have a personal encounter with a living God. In becoming a fully devoted follower of Jesus, girls have the chance to participate in a relationship of personal love and forgiveness that totally rights the worst of the world's wrongs. Your girl can experience infinite forgiveness when the rest of the world would rather see her damned for her mistakes. A relationship with Jesus extends far beyond you, and in fact can serve to make right many of the wrongs you've committed or may yet commit. Jesus is the wellspring of love from which your girl can drink forever. He is the source of love that sets your girl apart and makes her a lifetime winner.

A relationship with Jesus is a dynamic adventure with endless possibilities. It costs nothing and in fact offers a gift as a reward. It's a gift that cannot be earned or made greater by the effort but is freely offered to those who ask and receive. The gift is the eternal presence of Jesus in your heart.

He becomes a constant companion and eternal friend, and his love is a gift poured out from a bottomless sea of grace. Girls who accept the gift cannot lose it under any circumstances, no matter how bad they are, no matter how far they drift, no matter what evil befalls them! He's the eternal safety net for girls living life on the ragged edge.

It doesn't matter if your daughter currently attends a church or synagogue, a mosque or temple, or no place of worship at all. What matters is the person to whom she gives her allegiance in faith. Since there is only one religion offering a living relationship, we think the inescapable option is Jesus.

Where Do We Get an Application?

How might we introduce Jesus to our girls? Serious devotion to Jesus can't be found in church. Applications aren't used in the kingdom. It's a relationship born in the heart and applied to life actively by faith in every breath you take. If you are serious about helping your girl become a fully devoted follower of Jesus, we strongly urge you to do three simple things.

- Get better acquainted with Jesus yourself
- Pray boldly for your daughter
- Do what he did

Get Better Acquainted with Jesus Yourself

This is really a simple matter. Even the most devout lifetime Christian can get better acquainted with the person of Jesus. The most devout lifetime atheist will find the introduction equally mesmerizing.

It is most effective to first introduce your daughter to some of the simpler things Jesus said and to all the miracles and remarkable things he did. The nature of his actions, parables, and stories say more about him than perhaps anything. These facts clearly reinforce and solidify his claim of being God and make it clear what a person needs to do to become a child of God. Your girl will need to take that step of faith herself and put her trust in Jesus. She will find this easier than you might think. Girls haven't developed reason extensively, and faith is much easier for those not so thoughtlessly addicted to reason. Reason, not religion, is the opiate of the American people. Radical faith begins with a simple request. It's as easy as having her close her eyes and say, "Jesus, come into my heart." We know it sounds too easy, but we didn't make the rules! Remember, divine occupancy is free. There's nothing required; no applications and no payments needed.

Next, let her get to know him. This happens by hearing what he said and did and by praying. Your girl can become thoroughly acquainted with Jesus through the first four Gospels of the New Testament. Those are the actual notes taken on Jesus' life. The clearest presentation of who he is and what he did can be found there. There are numerous versions of the Bible specifically for children. After reading the Gospels she will want to delve further into the mysteries of Jesus found in the rest of the Bible.

Pray Boldly for Your Daughter

Let's talk just a bit about prayer. Jesus spent the early morning hours of each day out away from others, praying. Prayer must be so important that we should begin the day with it. What did Jesus pray for? To do his Father's will, for the faith of his followers, and for spiritual strength. Seeing the success of his work and the magnitude of his impact, we know his prayers were effective. Maybe we too ought to fervently pray for those things that concern us.

We highly recommend prayer on two distinct fronts. First, you as a parent should spend time praying specifically for your girl. Pray for your daughter's faith. Pray for her health, friends and enemies, her opportunities, safety, self-control, resilience, sense of humor, teachers, and her judgment. Pray for your own wisdom in handling complicated life situations. Praying for her makes you better parents. Prayer builds your faith and confidence. Prayer is a place of solace and care you can retreat to when times get tough. Times will get tough (but God is listening).

Let her know that you are praying for her.

The second prayer front is teaching her to pray on her own. God listens when nobody else will. He is always there to hear teary confessions, pleas of help, requests for guidance, cries of loneliness.

We're a little hesitant to suggest that you use the canned "Now I lay me down to sleep . . ." but for some girls that is a great place to begin to learn to pray. Wherever prayer life begins is a good place. Teach your girl to just talk to God. Since he's now a local resident it makes sense to consult with him, confide in him, laugh, cry, scream, and dance with him. What a friend! What a comforter! This is a magnificent, twenty-four-hour-a-day friend, counselor, and faith generator! What is important for your daughter to recall is that she's not communing with a distant, ethereal deity but a living person who wishes more than anything to have a relationship with her.

If you prefer to teach her other prayers, please feel free. Perhaps the following prayer is one you could do with her and practice daily. Add or subtract as you feel the need:

Dear Jesus, I want to thank you for so many things! I know you are in heaven listening to me, and I thank you for being my God and promising me a future in your kingdom. Let me know what I need to do to work into your plans. Thank you for the food you've given us today, our home, clothes, and friends; and forgive me for anything mean I did today. Help me to forgive anybody who did anything wrong against me today, because it's hard for me to forgive people by myself. Help me to know right from wrong, and protect me against bad things and bad people. Thank you for being my friend forever and ever and promising that our friendship will never end. Amen.

What you are trying to do here is build a foundation of dynamic, lively faith. That takes time and effort. The need for faith has never been more pressing. Faith grows by learning more about God and practicing trust in him. Help your girl use prayer as a means to practice her faith.

Do What He Did

In three short years, Jesus turned the world solidly on its ear. To call his life an adventure is to vastly underrate what he accomplished. Oh that any of us could have a billionth of the impact and a trickle of the excitement he created!

Every girl likes real-life high drama and adventure. She'll find that living a life like Jesus lived is real adventure. He treated others as he wished to be treated. He confronted his critics, did numerous miracles, healed the sick, raised the dead! This man makes Indiana Jones look like a wimp. And he made a curious promise: He said that those who were his followers would do all he did and more! If we live by the promise that whatever God did for anyone in the Bible, he will do for us, some dynamic opportunities are opened up.

Here's where your faith *really* gets tested. The basic concept for building a girl who lasts through the tough times is helping her develop a living faith like that of believers in the Bible. A window-dressed faith can't conquer the mean streets of life. A living faith can dream and strive, can get up when knocked down, can laugh and dance! Faith that isn't lived is philosophy. Choose the lively alternative.

The Bible is a catalog of ordinary people doing extraordinary things. Its pages are filled with miraculous deeds performed by simple people acting on their faith in God. Their faith was alive, and their deeds proved it. These people are our role models of action.

Familiarize your daughter with the people of the Bible and the things they did. Find a Bible that lists all their great feats, or find a book that breaks down the stories into children's language. Read them, speak them, and live them in front of your girl. And always remind her that whatever God did for any of those people in those stories, he will do for her today.

Make faith tangible. Let her see your faith in action and encourage her to put her faith to the test. Faith does not grow hanging in a cedar closet waiting to be worn once in a while like a party dress. Faith grows by practice. At first she may be able to trust only for small things, but as she sees God working, her faith will grow. That's exciting! It may be helpful for you and her to get to know someone whose faith is strong, someone who can show you what having faith in God looks like, someone who knows how to make doing what Jesus did a real thing!

We know a family who does this on a consistent basis. The father's business cycles wildly, and the downtimes are financially stressful. They've made it a family project to gather daily to pray for the father's business success. When he has a particularly successful week (which happens regularly), they celebrate the answered prayers! They get more excited about their prayers being answered than the fact that their dad is succeeding. That is a powerful, living example of faith in action. And this family could be the family living next door to you. Why, for that matter, this could be your family!

Say Good-Bye

Every day in this country, thousands of girls leave home to strike out on their own. That's really what all this is about, isn't it? Each of them has her own stories, her own worries and weaknesses, her own private plans and strengths, and her own special hopes and dreams. What they lack in knowledge and experience they'll make up for with excitement and imagination. Yet even with all that, life will nick and scrape them in countless ways. How they each will finally end up is a mystery.

As Mother Teresa said, "Where there is mystery, there must be faith." Keep your faith well kindled. Make it the foundation upon which you stand. One day soon she'll be gone, and you'll be left to remember the dolls, the dress ups, the dances, the boyfriends, the broken hearts, the happy thoughts, the warm times, and the concern you poured over her in love. It will all come into focus in that moment when you say good-bye.

Do your very best, then kiss her gently and let her go.

A Postscript
for Extra-Special Parents

Who Are the Extra-Special Parents?

Life in the latter part of this century hasn't been family friendly. Though the trend now appears to be changing, we've spent decades nonchalantly creating a deeply divided society. While we've toyed with various combinations of living and working arrangements, birth has continued and children's needs have cried out for attention. The social experimentation has been costly. We're only now beginning to realize the extent of the damage.

You extra-special parents are the assortment of people who have answered the needs created by this experiment. Single parents, stepparents, foster parents, and grandparents top the list. Each of these groups has special needs and concerns. Anybody within any of these arrangements can raise winning girls, but some special attention and focus will be very helpful.

Single Parents

You aren't alone. Yes, you do have your work cut out for you, but you *can* raise an extraordinary girl. Some of the most successful and happy women we know came out of broken homes. Though it's certainly better to have a home intact, a death or divorce is not the end of the success trail.

A number of considerations may be of help. First, girls simply need both men and women in their lives. You must do what you can to get your daughter exposed to both adult men and women. The contact is vital for her to learn social roles and the habits and styles of each gender. Second, be careful to speak well of people of the opposite sex. Divorces are usually nasty, painful situations made even more regrettable by your own bitterness and sense of failure. Do all you can to shield your daughter from your own natural anger toward the opposite sex or disillusionment with the institution that unites the sexes, marriage.

We hold marriage in a place of sacred honor. We feel that marriage is normal and desirable and that committing to it is something healthy people do. But healthy people have marriages that blow up or partners who die. Let's make extreme efforts to soften the blow on our girls and encourage them that marriage is good. Be supportive and optimistic about your girl being happy with a member of the opposite sex.

Third, get yourself and your girl involved with other families as quickly as possible. We understand that single parents often feel ostracized by others and feel as if they don't fit into group situations. In spite of that, it's important for your daughter to be exposed to families where both parents are present. School and church activities are good places for this interaction to take place.

If your daughter has no siblings, it will benefit you both to become involved with other families like yours. Parents without partners groups are good settings for this. You can also ask other single parents about social functions in the area and consult bulletin boards at the library or at work. If you don't have a family, create one!

If you've survived a divorce, you know many things about pain and disappointment. As a final thought let us underscore that single parenthood needn't stop you from fully and energetically pursuing a great life with your girl. Keep your chin up and do what you must to buoy your confidence and optimism. Your girl will be fine if you continue to be active in life and attack your situation boldly.

Stepparents

If you're a stepparent, nobody envies you, and we needn't tell you why! You probably don't envy yourself! Stepparents tend to be either heroes or villains. You're a hero if you come into a bad situation with optimism and hope. You're considered a hero if your new spouse thinks you are the greatest and the kids readily accept and love you. You may be considered a villain, though, if you have married into a difficult situation. Perhaps the kids have been emotionally damaged and are unable to feel anything but contempt and hate. Perhaps there's an ex-spouse who causes pain and destruction for the family. The lives of these groups of stepparents could not be more radically different from each other.

If the former is your case, please bow your head now and thank God. There are several million other adults out there, married, remarried, or divorced, who would gladly trade shoes. If you are one of the "villains," some simple ideas might help. The enormous problems you face cannot be cured within the span of a few paragraphs. It would be very common for your situation to be so confusing that only outside consultation could sort it out. Don't feel bad about that, but confidently pursue it should it be the right course. Short of that, however, consider these ideas.

You cannot change the fact that the kids have been through a lot. They're like wounded animals, who bite anyone who gets too close, even someone who's trying to help. So though you may have a mind to venture in and get cozy with them, we suggest that you wait patiently and control the only element you can successfully control: you!

Be kind and supportive, firm and resolute. Very few successful stepparents are successful right from the start. They build success over time. Commit yourself to being fair-minded and confident and above all else committed to making a good life for everyone, no matter what they think of you. Pray for your own patience and resolve, for your spouse, and for the kids, too. Don't let their words or actions dissuade you from your mission of excellence. That is all you can control, so do it well.

Expect the girls to experience wide mood swings. Girls, especially older girls, are most likely going to swing unpredictably between liking you and defending you to seeing you as a divisive threat and an irritating flake. Stay the course. Don't allow your stepdaughter's moods to dictate your actions. Set the tone yourself and stick to it. Remain firmly optimistic.

Don't let the difficulty bury you. There are good times, and plenty of stepparents have grown enormously satisfying home lives. It just takes time, patience, and dedication. Put your heart and soul into it, and be clearly intent on winning your new home. Fight with love and perseverance, and you will win.

Foster Parents

Our hearts are with you. You've taken a big, selfless risk in assuming responsibility for a young life. Your attachment to your girl is complete, and biology matters little in the tie that binds you together. You've been selfless, and your rewards will be great. Until the awards ceremony comes, however, here are some thoughts.

Your kids need lots of love and patience. All foster children have special needs. It may be because of developmental or medical problems. It may be because they are foreign born, are older children, or have behavior problems. Your foster child entered your life with a complete set of luggage from a previous life. All you can initially offer them, regardless of their age, is acceptance and protection. As time goes by, let your acceptance build into love, and let your protection of them build into patience as they sprout and grow under your tutelage. It may be slow and it may be hard, but remain committed to them in love, and patiently take them forward. You are doing a job few others would even consider. Thank-you.

Grandparents

You've already been around the parenting merry-go-round once, so go ahead and admit it; you'd rather not have to ride it again! But like it or not, odd circumstances prevail, and you find yourself parenting again.

Regardless of why you are parenting grandchildren, the situation will be difficult and the children will have been through a lot. But let's face it; you didn't get to be grandparents without winning in a few bad situations. You're a hero, like it or not.

By virtue of your natural authority and constancy in your grandchildren's lives, many of the control issues of other extra-special parent relationships are absent. That doesn't mean, however, that you won't have general incorrigibility to deal with, or even worse dilemmas.

The biggest complaint we hear from grandparents parenting again is about the amount of stamina required. You have kids who not only need your support and direction but also have the energy to light your house for a year. One of the most serious recommendations we can make is that you get in shape and take vitamins. These are excellent steps that simply make sense.

We also strongly recommend finding a support group. You need fresh ideas and encouragement. Your local chapter of the American Association of Retired People, schools, libraries, and social service organizations maintain a list of such groups in your geographical area. You will find that swapping ideas with other grandparents who are parenting is eye-opening and encouraging. It may even embolden you to take on your responsibility with some vigor. We've heard of some individuals looking on the opportunity of raising grandchildren as a way to right some of the wrongs of their first round of childrearing. However you conceive of it, you are contributing to the health and stability of the next generation of your family. This is no light matter; what you do is of life and death proportions for your family.

Of course it's rough. Naturally it's exhausting. We're sure it's confusing. But press on! You can and you must. Somehow, someway it will work out! The next generations will say thanks.

Notes

1. Deborah Tannen, *You Just Don't Understand: Women and Men in Conversation* (New York: Ballantine, 1990), 25.

2. Ibid., 52.

3. Louisa May Alcott, *Little Men* (Boston: S. J. Parkhill and Co., 1871), 40–43.

4. Desmond Doig, *Mother Teresa: Her People and Her Work* (New York: Harper and Row, 1976), 31, 54.

5. Joni Eareckson Tada, *Secret Strength . . . For Those Who Search* (Portland: Multnomah, 1988), 334–35.

6. Sarah and A. Elizabeth Delany, *Having Our Say: The Delany Sisters' First 100 Years* (New York: Kodansha America Inc., 1993), 154–55.

7. Corrie ten Boom, *The Hiding Place* (New York: Bantam, 1971), 238.

8. Brian Lanker, *Portraits of Black Women Who Changed America* (New York: Stewart, Tabori, and Chang, 1989), 66.

9. Maria Montessori, *The Absorbent Mind,* trans. Claude A. Claremont (New York: Holt, Rinehart, and Winston, 1967), 4.

10. Libby Riddles and Tim Jones, *Race Across Alaska: First Woman to Win the Iditarod Tells Her Story* (Harrisburg, Pa.: Stackpole Books, 1988), 137.

11. Alcott, *Little Men,* 353.

12. Eugene H. Peterson, *The Message* (Colorado Springs: NavPress, 1993), 424–25.

William Beausay is a licensed psychotherapist, speaker, and corporate consultant with his organization WINNERS! **Kathryn Beausay** is a speech and language pathologist. Kathryn lives in Toledo, Ohio, with their three kids, Jake, Jessie, and Zac.

William Beausay is a licensed psychotherapist, speaker, and corporate consultant with his organization WINNERS! Kathryn Beausay is a speech and language pathologist. The Beausays are parents of two sons and one daughter.

For information regarding books, seminars, workshops, keynotes, the "Winners! Series" of audiotapes, or other personal appearances, write us at:

Winners!
209 E. Dudley
Maumee, OH 43537

E-mail us at:

winners@cris.com

or call:

419-893-1983

Watch for the **Winners! Homepage** on the **Worldwide Web,** starting the summer of 1996.